WOODCRAFT

WOODCRAFT

A Guide to Using Trees for Woodcraft and Bushcraft

JOHN RHYDER
Foreword by BEN LAW

To my wife Caron, who is a constant help, support and inspiration in all I do, and my son Finn, who inspires me with his own determination, morality and unique view of the world.

First published in Great Britain by Practical Nature, 2018
© text and images John Rhyder, 2018
All photographs by John Rhyder and Caron Buckingham-Rhyder

Reprinted 2022

The History Press
97 St George's Place, Cheltenham,
Gloucestershire, GL50 3QB
www.thehistorypress.co.uk

British Library Cataloguing in Publication Data.
A catalogue record for this book is available from the British Library.

ISBN 978 0 7509 9818 5

Typesetting and origination by The History Press
Printed and bound in Turkey by Imak.

Contents

Acknowledgements

I THANK ALL THOSE countrymen, naturalists and woodsmen who taught me so much that I needed to learn. First, for my earliest lessons, my father, followed by a succession of those I call 'the old boys'. In truth, when we met, they were not much older than I am now, and sadly most have now gone. So, to Harold, Fred, Ron, Ginge and Andy: thanks for everything.

A big thanks to Phil Brooke for supporting Woodcraft School over the last several years, and for starring in many of the images in this book. Also, thanks to Warren Frost for colour balancing and general help with the photography, and for the plan drawings of the bow designs.

Foreword

AS A WOODSMAN, I have to admit to being tempted by the ever-increasing variety of tools and equipment that is available for working with wood and it is refreshing to be reminded of the simplicity of the proverb 'a few tools and a wide range of skills can achieve many things'.

In *Woodcraft*, John Rhyder encourages us to fell, shape and make a variety of craft with a few tools and to learn the core skills of reading a tree, understanding its history and growth and then safely felling it.

With the tree felled John guides us through a range of crafts made from the wood, the roots and the bark. Core woodsman skills of identification of fungi and fire-making are all here and blended with stories and observations from John's many years of wildlife tracking and ethnobotanical research. He starts with simple projects to get you used to your tools like feathering sticks for firelighting, through spoon carving, weaving bark and then onto more challenging projects like making a bow. John's passion and knowledge of bow-making shines through and the detail in choosing the right piece of wood, the balance of the bow and then making the bow-string, arrows and quiver reconnects us to our ancestral heritage.

So much of this book is about learning traditional skills, making items rather than buying them, and in turn allowing us to reconnect with a way of thinking, being and working that we are sadly losing touch with.

In a time where many of us are reassessing our lives, looking for more meaning than staring at a computer screen day after day, taking a journey with John into 'woodcraft' could be the start of reconnecting with nature and finding more balance and well-being in our view of the world.

Ben Law

Introduction

I WAS OUT TRAILING a roe deer this morning, trying my best to stay on its track as it meandered under low branches and through thickets. Our route was criss-crossed with the trails of numerous other animals including badgers, other roe deer and, at one point, the unmistakable pattern of a mountain biker's tyres. It occurred to me that not so long ago, our total dependence on the natural world would have meant that each of us would have had a similar experience to this.

This dependence on the earth's resources hasn't changed: we are still able only to utilise the wealth of one planet. Unfortunately, most people's lives are so far removed from this concept that the word 'divorced' doesn't do them justice – many haven't even got as far as divorce, they probably missed not only the wedding, but the first date. Awareness of our natural surroundings is lost as an unfortunate side-effect of the modern age. This is not just a shame but, I believe, deeply damaging to the human body and psyche, which evolved in the midst of nature.

I read somewhere a while ago that animals release endorphins when engaged in what we see as instinctual behaviour. This makes evolutionary sense: pleasure is given as a reward for behaviour that leads to success, and successful behaviour becomes pleasurable, and so it continues. To put it another way, badgers love digging: take away the need for a badger to dig by giving it a home and food, and it still digs. The badger gets a kick out of digging, and carries on doing so, even when it is no longer necessary to meet its basic survival needs.

Roe deer.

We are tool-using hominids who evolved outdoors surrounded by nature, so it seems obvious why being outside and making connections with nature would appeal to so many of us. I'm guessing that anyone who has read this far would, like me, not miss a chance to track and watch animals, experiment with wild food, or just marvel at a tree or mountain. Throw in the chance of making something and our 'badger endorphins' will be really flowing. Nature rewards this behaviour, which we were once so dependent on, by making it pleasurable. However, the pleasure goes much further than simple survival requires – which is why art and craft have gone far beyond the practical, all the way back into prehistory.

The techniques I describe in this book require only simple tools, so a workshop full of gadgets – in this gadget-dependent world – is unnecessary. Familiarity with a few trusted tools and the skill to use them are the key, despite the generally accepted assumption that buying the latest and most expensive tool will make us magnificent craftsmen. (Please note that, in this book, the traditional terms woodsman and craftsmen apply equally to women as to men.) I also suggest that, since these techniques are dependent on few tools, they can be used even in remote areas.

However, remember those endorphins: you don't need to be in a survival situation to enjoy woodcraft. Please don't be concerned that you are living a fantasy or having a Davy Crockett moment. I have been lucky enough to fell trees with axes in the Arctic Circle while balancing on unfamiliar skis. I have carved spoons in a snowstorm and played around with all manner of natural materials in all kinds of unlikely situations. It really doesn't matter whether or not you're doing the same. Develop your skills outdoors if you can, but the techniques are every bit as useful in your garden, garage or on the dining room floor. It doesn't matter, it's what you were designed to do.

This volume focuses on some bushcraft or woodcraft skills specifically associated with trees and timber. I have picked techniques, materials and projects that I consider to be the most closely linked to those of the woodsman. Please don't be upset if your craftwork doesn't immediately hit gallery standards. There will always be those who are so talented that anything they make is of exceptional quality. I certainly don't put myself in that category: I have always had to work very hard to achieve anything remotely artistic. The more you practise, the easier these things become.

If you are keen on bushcraft, then being good in the woods isn't just about making things; however, this is no more a bushcraft book than it is a woodworking guide. Instead, I explore the possibilities that trees offer to the woodsman, and the places where knowledge of tools and materials can lead. With that in mind, I have not offered hundreds of craft projects. Rather, those I have described are included to help you develop your knowledge of techniques and materials, leading you on to finer and more complex endeavours.

I believe that some elements of woodcraft are relatively simple to understand, and probably can be mastered with experience acquired through experimentation; these have been given less attention. Other elements, such as bow-making, are explored in greater detail; it is something that links together many skills, with the craftsman required to fell, cleave and shape their material, and to be sufficiently accurate in all this work that the wood can be bent and released many thousands of times without breaking.

In writing this book, I had no desire to recreate the works of other people. My intention was not to wax lyrical about the various methods of making fire, describe hypothermia, explain first aid or help you choose a sleeping bag. Important though these things are to any serious student of bushcraft, they have all been described more than adequately elsewhere.

Instead, I have tried to write from my own experience of teaching and practising these skills. I hope, as a result, that you find this book fresh and compelling.

John Rhyder, Sussex, UK

Note on Measurements

Many traditional skills and crafts are expressed in old imperial measurements, especially subjects such as bow-making. Throughout the book I have endeavoured to convert imperial to metric, although oftentimes this is an approximation. A millimetre or two here and there should not really make much difference to the craft process.

1

Felling and Harvesting

I guess the pinnacle of my tree-working career was on what is euphemistically called a 'crane job'. These involve, due to constraints either of time or access, climbing the tree that is to be felled. Once you're up the tree, all the branches are severed and lowered by crane, followed by the crown, and finally the trunk, section by section. When all the branches have gone, the climber – in this instance, yours truly – is left standing in climbing spikes, tied around the main trunk and unable to get out of the way. As you may imagine, the climber is then wholly dependent on the crane operator swinging the severed lumps smartly away, to avoid smearing said climber up and down what remains of the trunk.

Unfortunately, in this case, my driver was a complete idiot. He seemed to delight in allowing 3-ton lumps of timber to crash back against the pole I was tied to. This demanded some smart dancing out of the way, followed by frantic hugging of what was left of the tree, as my climbing spikes popped out. I am told I seemed less than impressed – and may even have sworn at the crane driver once or twice!

However, the final straw came later when I was back on the ground. The driver was moving some of the timber around when, with no warning, the strop that, only minutes before, was holding heavy timber inches from my head, suddenly broke.

Think first aid whenever you are out felling.

Felling

Felling trees can be, and often is, difficult and dangerous. Even with a relatively small tree, things can go disastrously wrong. The beauty of cutting trees for bushcraft is that you can choose. You don't have to fell difficult and dangerous trees – those trees that are liable to split, or get badly stuck, or fall the wrong way and break something you would rather have kept intact. You are unlikely to have to fell a tree of legendary proportions, either.

For bushcraft, we are generally dealing with trees of a slightly more genial disposition than those the average forester or arborist has to work with. Nonetheless, you still need to be mindful and follow a few simple guidelines – even a relatively small and humble-looking tree can bite you on the backside if you get things wrong.

Initial Tasks
Felling trees involves a few initial routine tasks. You must have the land-owner's permission before you start work, and you should get to grips with the following:

- tree preservation orders

- conservation areas

- sites of special scientific interest, and other protected areas

- the effects that your activities might have on watercourses and archaeological sites.

Top-to-Toe Survey

It is critically important to evaluate the condition of any tree that you are about to fell, to ensure it doesn't surprise you on the way down. Certain structural defects have a habit of making trees do the unexpected, so keep a look out for any major deadwood or hanging branches, and note the presence of fungal bodies, cavities and tight forks. All of these may cause the tree to break out as it moves.

Start at the top of the tree and work your way down to the root area. Take note of any swelling on the butt of the tree, or excessive root buttresses. In conifers, uniform swelling across the butt of the tree can indicate butt rot, which causes the centre of the tree to decay. This swelling – also known as 'bottle butt', as it can leave a tree resembling a wine bottle – is a sign that the tree is trying to compensate for its weakness by producing more wood. Excessively large buttress roots also might be a sign of trees that are compensating for decay low down; but be aware that trees will also do this to anchor themselves on exposed sites and against the prevailing wind. (Incidentally, this can make them a useful feature for natural navigation.) Felling is much trickier when a tree is decayed. There are examples of many of these features in Chapter 8.

As woodsmen, we have a duty to the rest of the animal kingdom, some of whom may have set up residence in our chosen tree. Look for signs of birds' nests, dormice and bats. Any budding lumberjack who disturbs the last two (or any specifically protected species of bird) or wilfully destroys their place of refuge is liable to a heavy fine – and quite right too. Ignorance is no defence in the eyes of the law, so it is up to you to be certain that you can identify the presence of such creatures. Depending on where you live, there may be a multitude of wildlife, some protected and some not, that you need to familiarise yourself with, but what a wonderful opportunity this is to get to grips with a few new species.

It is important to check the neighbouring trees for everything mentioned above, especially if they are likely to be disturbed by your tree as it falls. Moreover, check any obvious hazards, such as power cables, in the vicinity.

Establishing Direction of Fall

Several factors influence where the tree will fall, but essentially you should look carefully at the tree to assess where it would fall if gravity alone took it to ground, then balance this against the spot where you would like it to fall.

Tools of the trade: bow saw, felling lever, homemade wedge, rope and throw line.

'Sod's law' clearly states that these two spots are unlikely to be the same, so a little tree-felling trickery with rope, wedges and other felling aids may be necessary. Where you want the tree to end up is likely to be an open area, for ease of processing and to reduce the chances of the tree getting stuck in another tree, or falling on your car (or worse still, your sandwiches).

Many people focus on the branching habit of the tree as the main criterion when choosing direction of fall. While it is true that a tree is more likely to fall to the side with the most limbs, you also should assess the orientation of the trunk. Bends and kinks in the main trunk can have the effect of pulling the tree against the weight of the branches or making it behave like a completely straight specimen. If the trunk bends in unison with the weight of the branches, the tree may start to fall much sooner than you anticipate, and with greater force and speed.

The final factor when selecting direction of fall is the wind. Wind can seriously undermine your best felling efforts, leading to embarrassing and potentially dangerous results. Even the professionals avoid felling if they cannot guarantee direction due to the wind (or at least, they are supposed to). Those who ignore the wind spend a good deal of their lunch hour wrestling trees to the ground, repairing sheds and fences (and eating very flat sandwiches).

Keeping Safe
Once the direction of fall has been established, the next step is to identify your danger zones, safe working areas and escape routes. The danger areas when felling a tree are directly behind the intended direction of fall, and directly in front. This leaves two escape routes and work areas, approximately 45° from the intended felling direction, at the sides of the tree.

You need to stick to these areas for working and step into them as the tree falls; therefore, they should be clear of any obstructions and trip hazards for at least 6–10ft (2–3m). In addition, you should carefully examine the line of fall and remove any potential future hazards. These generally include small saplings and coppice stools (the stumps from which new growth appears), which may be put under severe tension by the grounded tree, and thus be dangerous when cut.

I once worked with a guy who had to have his nose reconstructed after he cut a hazel wand he hadn't noticed, which was now trapped under a tree: the wand sprang back and hit him full in the face.

It is important to establish a clear work area – a safe zone – around the tree that is to be felled. The axe indicates the direction of fall.

Felling a tree correctly is all about control. To put it another way, you should know exactly what the tree is likely to do through the whole process, and not be taken by surprise. Assuming that there are no obvious obstructions and without adverse wind conditions, all a tree needs to do is tip past the vertical far enough for gravity to take over.

Ideally, a tree should fall when you decide to tip it past its point of balance using one of the felling aids described later (see p.34). However, a tree that is leaning, a particular orientation of branches and trunk or, indeed, one with some wind behind it, may fall before you have a chance to tip it forwards. This is not a problem, so long as you are aware that it is about to happen.

! Remember: control is about not being taken by surprise and being able to predict what will happen.

We have already mentioned some further exceptions, as well as the risk of a tree falling early, to being in control. It is difficult to deal with wind, for example, or a tree that is heavily weighted towards the direction of fall. The latter is exceptionally problematic if you are using hand tools, and the surest way to cut it with any degree of safety or predictability is by using a chainsaw. Trees heavily weighted in the direction of fall are liable to split alarmingly, causing what is known as a 'barber chair'.

This tree almost split because it fell early on too wide a hinge. This is close to becoming a 'barber chair'.

For our bushcraft purposes, I strongly recommend you avoid such trees – with inexperience and hand tools, they are very dangerous. I won't give you any more detail here, but there are lots of examples of barber chairs on the internet if you do want to find out more.

Think it Through, and Take a Break

There are, no doubt, those among you who would infer from some of my earlier comments an obsessive interest in lunch hours and sandwiches. This isn't necessarily the case – but I would just say that virtually all the accidents I have experienced or witnessed have occurred when a break was imminent. Thinking about felling just one more tree before lunch often leads to bad decisions or a lapse in concentration.

I advise you to take regular breaks that will give you thinking time and help you to avoid mistakes caused by fatigue. Never go felling on your own; instead, try to develop a buddy system, so that you can watch out for signs of fatigue and frustration in each other.

The Felling Cuts

There are several things we need to be aware of when cutting a tree. Each of them has a huge bearing on how, when and under how much control the tree falls. I will cover these below, but I should also point out that most of the following photographs show trees felled with a chainsaw. This is because the size and precision of the kerf (the slot left by the saw blade) created by a chainsaw shows the process in greater detail than when hand tools are used.

Many readers will be familiar already with the main felling cut. It is variously called a 'frog cut', 'sink cut', 'gob cut' or 'face cut', as well as having the more long-winded name, 'directional felling cut' (and doubtless several other regional names). As the last name suggests, this cut is responsible for the general direction that the tree falls after taking into account wind and lean. I will describe it as the sink cut from now on.

!   Remember: it doesn't matter how accurate your cutting is if the sink cut is put in an unrealistic position in relation to the weight of the tree. The depth of a sink cut is generally one-fifth to one-quarter of the overall diameter of the tree, and normally the angle is set at 45°.

The second cut you'll need to make is known as the 'back cut'. It is placed in line with, or slightly above, the back of the sink, leaving a 'hinge' of uncut wood that is about 10 per cent of the diameter of the tree. As the name suggests, this piece of uncut wood allows the tree to fold over in a similar way to a door hinge. It is worth remembering that this hinge provides the only real control you have over the fall of the tree.

Variations are always possible on the position and dimensions of these cuts – with associated consequences. I am going to explore them a little further, as some might be useful, and some might explain why you have just broken a favourite piece of kit that you thought you'd neatly left in a safe place.

While the sink cut is normally set at 45°, there can be considerable variety in the angle to suit different situations. Understanding the function of the sink makes this clearer. Together with giving direction, the sink controls when the hinge breaks and the tree goes into free fall. Essentially, the tree will be separated from its stump when the faces of the sink cut meet.

It is worth noting here that there are always exceptions: some really fibrous species of tree hold to their stump almost regardless of the chosen sink angle. However, in most cases, the more open the sink cut, the closer to the ground the tree will be before it breaks off. This can be very useful for control, especially if there is a slight wind or the tree is likely to hit an obstacle on its way to the ground. Moreover, it can be helpful if there is any chance of the tree rolling once it has hit the ground, as it is quite possible to have the tree down and still attached to the stump, which makes general delimbing much easier. The downside to an open sink is that a good deal more timber is removed, effectively wasting more of the butt end of your tree.

By contrast, if the sink angle is lower than 45°, the tree will break off early. This can be useful when you are felling over immovable obstacles, such as banks or log stacks. In this instance, when the tree begins to freefall it is able to roll over the obstacle, reducing the likelihood of the butt being smashed, which would be both dangerous and wasteful. As a bonus, you will also have removed a smaller piece of the butt, thus being left with more timber.

normal, well-proportioned sink cut, with a level back cut and perfect hinge.

Sometimes marking where the back cut will go can improve accuracy.

This tree is still attached to the stump as a result of an open sink cut.

! Remember: an intact hinge is really the only control you have over the tree, and once the hinge is severed, the trunk will go where wind and gravity take it.

The two cuts that make up the sink must meet exactly, otherwise you may be undermining the hinge, so consider marking the position of your cuts prior to beginning work.

Although the sink gives the tree's direction of fall, it is important to understand that this only happens in conjunction with a level and parallel hinge. If the hinge is left thicker on one side than the other, the tree is likely to be pulled to that side. Similarly, if the hinge is uneven in height, because either the back cut or the sink are not perpendicular to the trunk, the tree is likely to pull to the side where there is more wood. With experience, this knowledge can be used to compensate for excessive sideways lean, but this requires a good deal of experience in both felling and how different species behave. Always remember that when searching for craft materials, we don't have to fell the most difficult trees in the forest.

! Now, I know I am banging on about this, but it is important not to forget – once the hinge has been severed, the tree is at the mercy of wind and gravity.

24

Of the three main elements, the back cut is one that should never really be varied. It needs to be in line with, or (to allow for mistakes!) preferably slightly above the bottom of the sink cut. The key detail is that when putting in the back cut, sufficient hinge is left. As mentioned above, this is normally 10 per cent of the overall diameter. If the hinge is too thin, control is lost; if it is too thick, the tree may not fall at all. A hinge that is too thick might even cause the tree to split into the stump and it will just rock backwards and forwards in a most embarrassing fashion.

There are other relationships between the various elements that should be considered. The depth of the sink can be vital, especially when using a wedge as a felling aid. Remembering that, all else being equal, a tree has to tip past

You can alter the angle of your sink cut to achieve slightly different results.

the vertical to fall, so sometimes driving a wedge into the back cut can help lift the tree. If the sink is too deep, you might find yourself already banging the wedge against the back of the hinge before the tree has tilted far enough to fall.

On a more fundamental level, if a tree is decayed, it is possible for it to fall due to a sink that is too large before the back cut has been made. (I know this because it happened to me while doing professional tree work, there was much hilarity at my expense, as I had to leap smartly out of the way.)

A similar problem can occur when the back cut is made lower than the back of the sink. The tree might then have to be lifted up and over the step that is formed before it can fall, which, again, may lead to the tree splitting into the stump and not falling.

Clockwise from top left: This hinge is much too thin, which may cause the tree to free fall; The hinge here is much too thick, which will cause wood to tear out, split or even form a 'barber chair'; An error that is very common when using a saw: the hinge is too thick in the middle, which has been caused by rolling the blade. This can make it hard to tip the tree; The hinge is uneven, causing the tree to pull to one side.

Hung-Up Trees

No matter how experienced you may be, and no matter how careful you are when felling, at some time or another you will get a tree stuck in another tree. It is important to have a few techniques up your sleeve for dealing with this eventuality safely, so you can avoid either breaking something or seriously hurting yourself. It is also wise to think about the consequences of various 'good' ideas that may occur to you as a way of solving this problem.

I have seen all of the following tried, with different degrees of danger and hilarity. So, listed in order of peril, avoid the following ways to get your hung-up tree down (indeed, if you are at all tempted to try anything listed below, stop, have a cup of tea and a serious chat with yourself):

- climbing up the tree and bouncing around on it or grabbing hold of it to give it a good wobble

- felling the tree in which your tree is hung up

- felling a neighbouring tree on top of your tree, in the vain hope that it will be dislodged

- when the last one doesn't work, felling a second or even a third tree – I have seen this done, and it became a very dangerous mess to sort out

- start hacking bits out of the bottom of the tree, in the hope that it will fall.

This last one is something that might be made to work, if you understand *why* it might be dangerous. If the felled tree is sitting at a steep angle, it is possible that chopping a few feet off the bottom end will result in the tree swinging in towards the tree in which it is hung up. It then can work itself free and fall back towards the tree-feller.

The general rule is that if the tree is standing at an angle of 45° or less, chopping a lump off the bottom will result in the tree hitting the ground and not swinging towards the tree-feller. In reality, while 45° is good as a rule of thumb, sometimes it is possible to cut pieces out of a tree at a steeper angle, provided that it can be clearly seen that the tree will hit the ground before it swings back. This sudden movement may be enough to dislodge the tree, but in any case, it will make the tree lighter, should it have to be poled or winched down.

As the hinge is still needed for control when you are taking down a hung-up tree, this is the prescribed method for dealing with the situation:

1. Assess the position and condition of the tree and its neighbours. Indeed, get into the habit of doing this every time a tree moves. Be on the lookout for hanging limbs up above, for small trees under tension, and for any sideways movement of the tree that might indicate the danger zones have changed.

!   Remember: the danger zones are always directly behind and in front of the likely tree fall.

2. Survey the tree. If it is to be rolled, which side should it be rolled towards – the right or the left, to make the tree most likely to fall to earth?

3. Prepare a new escape route, bearing in mind both the decision above and whether the tree has moved.

4. Check the condition of the hinge – is it intact and straight across the diameter of the tree in the correct direction?

5. Find or cut a stout pole, around 8ft (2.4m) in length (for reasons I will explain shortly).

6. Assuming the hinge is intact and that, for example, we are rolling the tree out towards the right, you need to cut away most of the hinge on the opposite side to the direction of roll. In this scenario, leave 20 per cent uncut on the right. To put it another way, remove 80 per cent of the hinge, leaving 20 per cent on the side you are rolling towards. Hopefully, the tree will pivot on the uncut portion of the hinge and fall, under control, to the ground.

Clockwise from above: Inspect the hinge. Options are limited if the hinge is not intact: here, I have removed some of the back of the tree to show the hinge better; Remove up to 80 per cent of the hinge; All being well, the tree will now roll out.

If the tree doesn't fall, then a felling lever – or in an emergency, a rope noose and pole, can be used to push the tree in the desired direction. If this fails too, the tree must be cut completely away from the stump and 'walked down' using the pole we cut earlier. (No doubt you were wondering when it would come in useful.)

The pole can be used to push the free tree off the stump if it doesn't immediately fall. In this instance, you must consider where the tree will land, once it is free of the stump: don't push off into a position where your tree might be forced into another obstruction. Sometimes a tree has to be walked an awfully long way before it falls, and it is all too easy to run out of room.

Whether you are rolling or walking a tree down, it is important to use the correct method to avoid straining your back or other injuries. Bend your knees, keep your back straight, and be sure to study the position of the pole in the photograph before you begin.

Left: Always push away from you when using a felling lever to roll a tree, to avoid bringing it down on top of you.

Above: Ensure that when a tree is pushed off its stump you are in an area where further takedown is possible. Using the pole like a battering ram helps to keep you safe.

Use the technique illustrated: if the tree falls suddenly and takes the pole down with it, the pole should fall between the legs of the operator. It is also easier to see the top and bottom of the tree and gauge its movement.

If you use the incorrect technique and the tree falls suddenly, the pole may fall across the legs of the operator.

If a tree is still hung up but off its stump, it can be walked down using a pole. The technique involves lifting and pushing away at the same time. You should place the pole as close to its end as you can, for better leverage.

Occasionally, despite your best efforts, nothing works, and the tree stubbornly remains standing. In such cases, mechanical methods must be employed, namely, winching.

Ropes can be also used to help bring down a hung-up tree in two ways:

1. If you have already used a rope as a felling aid, you can use the same rope to pull the tree over by partially severing the hinge and pulling at 90° to the direction of fall. In effect, you are using the rope as a felling lever.

2. If you haven't already used a rope for the felling, you can attach one using a 'carter's hitch' (for ropes and knots see Chapter 9), and use it to pull the tree backwards, once it has been freed from its stump.

! Beware: be extremely careful when attaching a rope to a hung-up tree, as you can easily find yourself not just in front of the tree, but also underneath it.

Of course, you are not obliged to fell every tree you come across. Be sure to avoid the most likely hang-up candidates, along with those trees that stay hanged. People, some of them very experienced, die regularly when working with timber.

Delimbing and Crosscutting
Before rushing in to delimb your felled tree, check the general area and ask yourself the following questions:

1. Is the tree truly on the ground? If not, is it likely to move suddenly?

2. If the tree isn't on the ground, have your safe areas changed? (The area directly behind your tree is still in the danger zone.)

3. Has the tree dislodged anything in neighbouring trees that is about to come crashing down?

4. Is the tree sitting on anything that may be under dangerous tension?

In fact, you need to ask these questions whenever your tree moves. Once you are satisfied that the area is safe, proceed with delimbing.

Removing the side branches and top of a felled tree, and crosscutting it to required lengths, requires an understanding of tension and compression. This knowledge is important to:

• avoid getting tools stuck

- understand how branches may spring, once severed

- avoid wasting timber by having the wood split as you release the tension.

In essence, tension is found on the outside edge of cut timber; put another way, the part of the wood that will open up if you cut through it with a saw. The compression wood is found on the inside edge of strained timber, and this will close the cut as you saw through, thus trapping the tool.

A useful way of visualising the tension is to imagine putting a huge force at the point where you want to place your cutting tool:

- If the wood is supported at both ends, it is likely that the top side will compress, and the underside stretch.

- If the wood is supported at one end, the opposite is likely to happen. (I use the word 'likely', because it is possible to have all sorts of side tension and compression with felled trees, so exact judgement can be tricky.)

I was once part of a three-man team that came to the aid of a colleague who had trapped his chainsaw while delimbing a large oak tree. I went in to free his saw, and promptly got mine trapped. We called for help and, you guessed it, trapped a third saw. It all looked quite attractive in a way, as the chainsaws were all the same model, and all arranged neatly in the wood. We could probably have sold a photo of them to the manufacturer for their catalogue.

In the end, we had to call in one of the old hands to free the saws, which he did with much smirking and many comments along the lines of 'boys at the game' and 'babes in the wood'. This does illustrate how awkward it can be to judge forces correctly.

When delimbing trees with axes, it makes sense to try to put the trunk of the tree between you and the sharp edge of your tool. Always work up the tree, from butt to crown, since this is an easier way to remove branches. Going from crown to butt is harder, because the branch collar is particularly tough in this direction, presumably because it has to deal with gravity weighing down each limb. Therefore, it makes sense to remove limbs from underneath; incidentally, this is also true for dealing with smaller stems with smaller tools, such as knives.

Unfortunately, this would also involve you walking backwards and jumping from one side of the tree to the other, something that is generally and rightly, frowned on by chainsaw users. However, if you are using hand tools, it can be perfectly safe – just so long as you clear as you go, take it steady, and make yourself aware of any possibility of the tree rolling as you flit, sylph-like, about the forest.

Try to remove all the branches flush to the stem, as any tiny twigs that stick out are likely to hinder stacking, rip up your hands and collect tool-blunting mud.

When you are crosscutting, you also will need to pay very close attention to the tension and compression within the tree. Crosscutting can be done fairly easily with an axe but, just as when you are felling, you will waste less wood using a saw. Cleanly sawn ends usually make further processing easier, especially when you have to split long lengths of wood down with wedges or stand short ones on stumps to make firewood. (For more on using tools, see Chapter 3.)

Felling Aids
Felling aids can be classed as anything that helps get a tree past its tipping point and merrily on its way down to earth. Key examples are felling levers, wedges, ropes and even winches.

Felling Levers
Essentially, a felling lever is inserted into the back cut, and the tree lifted from that point. Felling levers have limited use in terms of the size of tree that you can safely lift before running the risk of having your intestines appear on the outside of your body. They are great for smaller trees and are always handy when dealing with hung-up trees, as they normally come with a useful turning hook.

Choosing to use a felling lever is a bit counter-intuitive, as you will have to stand in the danger zone to lift your tree. Only use one to lift a tree when you have a hinge of correct and adequate dimensions (by then you are past the barber chair stage) and step smartly into your escape route as soon as the tree begins to fall.

Clockwise from right: Ensure the limb to be cut is behind your body; Swap sides as needed, to keep the tree between you and the axe; When in doubt, step further out to make sure your body is clear of the follow through.

Wedges

Wedges, whether bought or homemade, are used in a similar way. They are driven into the back cut to provide a good deal of lift. If you are making your own wedges, be sure to carve a long and even taper. Wedges with an obtuse angle are likely to bounce out of the cut.

Ropes

Felling levers and wedges are fine when a saw has been used to create the back cut. However, if you are felling with an axe, in effect two sink cuts are created. Unless there is an obvious lean to the tree, always use a rope instead.

In any case, I would suggest that occasional tree-fellers use ropes as a matter of course. They give both options and control, allowing the tree to be pulled without having to have anyone near the dangerous bit. In addition, they can be used to help down a hung-up tree by pulling in the direction of the roll-out.

Often, getting the rope high enough up the tree to make a difference can cause a few moments of head-scratching. Your first instinct may well be to tie something heavy (a shackle bolt is a favourite) to a light line and hurl it as hard and fast as possible into the canopy (no doubt accompanied by grunts and squeals to rival Wimbledon finalists). The shackle bolt invariably gets caught on something, either stuck or having to be pulled out so hard that it flies back at you at a speed that makes it impossible to avoid.

It's worth noting that shackle bolt meeting skull at a range of 30ft (10m) tends to hurt quite a bit. It is much easier to get the rope into your tree using a method from my tree surgery days. I believe it originated at my old college, Merrist Wood in Surrey, and I have always heard it referred to as the 'Merrist Wood missile'. It is still used by tree surgeons to access the canopy of trees and, coupled with a carter's hitch, gives great control over the fall (see ropes and knots in Chapter 9).

Opposite: Felling with an axe creates two sink cuts. If you don't use a rope, your tree may fall backwards.

Harvesting

Harvesting Smaller Trees

Taking down smaller trees, by which I mean trees 4–6in (10–15cm) (or even less) in diameter, is a lot less fraught than dealing with the big guys. However, for the larger of the smaller trees, it is still worth making the general safety assessment that we applied before.

Otherwise, sometimes it is easier to use a 'step cut', especially if the tree is likely to lean into other trees and then can be lifted out. Essentially, it involves cutting part-way through the stem on one side of the tree, then overlapping that cut on the opposite side, 2–3in (5–8cm) higher up. In principle, the tree can be gently rocked until the wood breaks along the grain between the two cuts.

As always, it is best to avoid any heavily leaning trees, and not to over-match yourself. A good rule of thumb is that if the tree is too heavy for you to lift, you should be using conventional felling cuts to make sure that you keep those intestines behind your stomach muscles. Everything is much neater that way.

Branches removed from trees that are to be retained can also be removed using step cuts, as there is less chance of the cut tearing down onto the tree.

L-R: To create a step cut, cut below first, then, overlapping, above; The stem should break off due to the grain splitting between the cuts; Finish off by pruning the stump.

Sustainable Harvesting

On our overcrowded island, it is vital that we are mindful of the impact that our activities have on the countryside. It is quite simple to make sure your activities have a neutral effect on woodland and, with a little thought, not especially hard to have a positive effect. Make sure you consider the following:

- where to take wood from

- how to remove stems and branches

- the species and form of the trees to be harvested.

Although woodland ecology and management is a fascinating subject – and I would encourage anyone to learn more about it – there isn't sufficient scope in this book to delve into the pros and cons of various woodland management systems. For me, walking through the woods and understanding what's going on only enhances my experience of the outdoors, so is worth studying just in that regard.

You don't have to be a professional forester to recognise that trees planted in neat rows, often all the same species, are likely to have been put there with a view to the landowner eventually felling them and making a few quid. Having you wade in and start knocking over potential bow staves won't do either you or the general image of the study of woodcraft much good, despite any permissions you might have. As mentioned previously, felling trees with bats, dormice or protected birds in them is legally and morally indefensible.

There are three harvesting principles that are relatively easy to get to grips with:

1. gathering from far and wide, when taking smaller numbers of trees

2. understanding ride management (see p.42) for larger amounts of wood

3. looking for suppressed trees.

1. *Coppicing*

When I teach this subject, it is normally at this point that I talk about coppicing, an ancient, early system of woodland management that is thought to reach back to the end of the Mesolithic period. When most of our hardwood (and some coniferous) trees are cut down, they respond by throwing out lots of shoots from dormant buds on the edge of the cut stump; a few send up shoots from the roots (technically, this is 'suckering', but the general effect is the same). In traditional coppice systems, these rods can be harvested at whatever size is convenient for any number of applications. In the days before power tools, it made sense to harvest wood at a useful size, rather than let it grow into big timber and then have to make it smaller using hand tools. It would appear that this cycle of felling and regrowth can be continued almost indefinitely.

For our purposes, the problem with coppicing is that it relies on large areas being cut, and often on some kind of protection from browsing animals for

Traditional coppicing relies on large areas being cut.

the regrowth. Like most flowering plants, our broadleaf trees require a good deal of sunlight to thrive – and cutting down large areas provides this. If we walk into a woodland and fell a tree in the middle of the forest or, equally, recut a coppice stool, it is very likely that the stool will be unable to regrow due to shade from its neighbours. If it does manage to regrow, its succulent new leaves become a magnet for lots of hungry deer and rabbits. If this young growth is repeatedly eaten, the tree may run out of stored energy and, its leaves having been sunlight-processing energy factories, find itself unable to replace that energy through photosynthesis. Cutting large areas negates the shade issue and, to some extent, stops the browsing by offering rabbits and deer such abundance that they can't possibly eat it all.

The upshot is that if you need a few hazel rods, for example, it is sensible to spread out your gathering by taking one rod from one stool and another from another stool. This way, you leave the bulk of energy-converting material firmly attached to the roots.

fresh, growing coppice stool will attract herbivores.

If a good deal of material is needed, you can't go far wrong by working on the edges of rides or tracks through the woodlands. These areas form an important transition between the shade of the forest and sunlit, open-edged habitat. In neglected woodland, these rides are generally the most recently open areas, and therefore have the most viable seed bank of wildflowers. It is often quite dramatic to open up a ride and see the variety of new growth that springs into life there.

2. Ride Management

Ride management essentially involves cutting back trees on either side of the track in a graded structure. Ideally a ride, or woodland edge of any kind, would have areas of bare earth, short sward, tall herbaceous plants, low canopy and high forest or tall, mature trees. The idea, together with letting in light, is to create structural diversity to suit a variety of different species. This structure can be mixed up: it is possible to have tall trees in the sward layer and coppice stools in the herbaceous layer.

The surface area of a ride can be increased by creating scallops, usually where trees are already a little thin on the ground; this also reduces any wind-tunnel effect.

Ride management encourages structural and species diversity.

3. Suppressed Trees

Another suitable type of tree to take is one that has been suppressed by its neighbours, trees that really have no chance of ever seeing the sky. Some sit under their bigger cousins for years, gradually weakening and dying. Such trees can be ideal for slightly bigger craft items, such as spoons and bowls.

Do gather responsibly, though, because today's suppressed tree is tomorrow's standing deadwood, which is an incredibly important ecological resource. Also, be aware that some tree species, among them beech, can tolerate being shaded for many years, and thus may not be as suppressed as they seem.

Pruning

Often, it is unnecessary to fell a tree completely: sometimes a branch is all that is needed for the work at hand. The way that you remove branches can have a huge influence on how a tree copes with the damage caused. It goes without saying that opening up the side of a tree exposes it to all manner of potential problems.

Fortunately, trees have evolved over millions of years to cope with damage and attacks by fungi, bacteria, animals – and the bushcraft community. However, the specific mechanisms that they have in place can be aided by the careful and considered actions of a respectful woodsman. Conversely, the wild swinging of a machete may result in problems to the tree long after the wielder has retired with a nasty (and no doubt well-deserved) blade-related injury.

It is worthwhile – as well as fascinating – to familiarise yourself with the arboricultural concept of Compartmentalisation of Decay in Trees (CODIT), a theory first described by American researcher Alex Shigo. Shigo looked at the way trees are able to lock out decay and prevent it from spreading, although it is now thought that the trees are more focused on limiting water-loss than decay.

In simple terms, a tree has several mechanisms that create barriers to the movement of decay organisms, so it's helpful to think of a tree in its proper three dimensions:

- The first barrier is blocking off vessels with chemicals and com-
  pounds that stop movement up and down the stem: 'tylosis'.

- The second barrier stops decay moving towards the centre of
  the tree by the annual rings.

- The third barrier is provided by medullary or wood rays, pre-
  venting the nasties from moving tangentially around the tree.

- The final barrier is, in essence, new wood produced in the
  cambium layer of the tree, which allows the tree to seal in any
  decay or damage.

Trees cannot heal their tissues; they can only seal off the problem. It is important never to remove the areas of the tree that contain the highest concentrations of cambium: namely, the branch and the root collars.

Opposite:
Clockwise from top left: The formation of this cavity was not stopped by tylosis; The skull and the dancing girl patterns show the trees' protective barriers; A branch collar cut; Leave the branch collar and sealing will occur.

2

Choosing and Maintaining Tools

It is written that, when one or more bushcraft practitioners are gathered together, they shall talk about knives. It's the one thing that we seem to get excited – and frankly opinionated – about. Whatever your own particular leanings are concerning sharp and shiny things, it's best to avoid those folks whose eyes moisten and glint alarmingly when Mick 'Crocodile' Dundee unsheathes his massive blade in the film *Crocodile Dundee*.

I simply recommend that any tool you pick is fit for service and in good order: I can well remember raising the shaft of a large axe to split some firewood, bringing it hurtling down on the wood, and being very surprised as the now extremely light shaft, minus its head, shattered on the block. Even more surprising was the distinct crash and tinkle of breaking glass from the greenhouse behind me ...

A confusing array of tools are available to the budding craftsman.

Choosing Your Tools

When I first became interested in woodcraft and traditional skills, I assumed that I would need specialist equipment to accomplish certain tasks. I soon realised that to complete craftwork, carvings and, in fact, all manner of wood-based projects, very little is actually required in the way of tools. It is true that certain tools will speed things up considerably, but this is of little importance to us as we're planning to make things in a non-commercial setting. The old cliché about enjoying the journey, rather than focusing on the destination, springs to mind here.

If you consider the coppice-workers of old, they were involved (in British woodland, in any case) in commercial activities. So, if you spend your whole day squaring up beams, it makes sense to have tools designed specifically for that task. Single bevel side-axes make perfect sense in this scenario. These blades remove wood in a similar way as a plane: the handles are often offset to keep your knuckles clear from the work.

However, everything made with a specialist axe (at least, everything that is described in this book) can be created with simple tools: it may just take a little longer to finish. Arguably, the same can be said of knives, indeed, of pretty much any woodworking tool. So, rather than promote the virtues of any specific tool, I have endeavoured to discuss the pros and cons of different types of tools to allow you to make a more informed choice when deciding what to buy.

is not necessary to use specialist tools, like this side axe, to create craftwork.

For me, the use of a few simple tools is one of the great joys of bushcraft. Below, I offer personal thoughts, based on my own preferences and experience, and therefore subject to my own bias. However, before I discuss tool types, there are a couple of generic considerations that apply equally to knives, axes and many other tools used in woodcraft: namely, bevel and steel choice.

Bevel Angle

It is useful to have a basic understanding of the various ways that cutting edges are set up. Without going into unnecessary detail, there are three principal level angles on cutting tools. The bevel is the part of the blade from the edge to the shoulder – the shoulder being the part where the blade starts when you are looking at it in cross-section. The way that these angles are arranged has a lot to do with strength and edge retention. A cutting tool with a flat-ground bevel has a reasonable amount of metal supporting the leading edge of the blade. Conversely, a convex bevel is rounded towards the leading edge of the blade, thus providing even more support to the edge.

For both types of bevels there can be considerable variation of angle. In essence, the more acute the angle, the better the slicing action, but this advantage comes at the expense of edge retention. The more obtuse the angle, the greater the edge retention at the expense of a clean slicing action, to the point that if the angle is too blunt the blade may not slice at all, instead splitting apart the material that is being cut. This may be useful on a log splitter, but it is not quite so helpful with an axe or a knife.

There is a third bevel angle commonly found on knives: the hollow ground version. This has a tiny secondary bevel, sitting on a concave bevel profile. Due to the concavity, there is very little material supporting the leading edge of the blade tip, which makes these types of bevel profile of little use for general carving. The thinness of the material may make them sharp but not especially robust.

However, for our purposes, realistically we have two options: convex or flat ground. Personally, I prefer a flat-ground bevel on a knife and would only use a convex bevel on an axe if it were either poor-quality metal or used exclusively for heavy splitting or felling work.

Even within the realms of the flat-ground edge, there are variations: many people recommend that tiny micro-bevels be added. It may be worth experimenting with this concept and, of course, finding out what your knife manufacturer recommends.

Stainless and Carbon Steel

While there is no need to become an expert metallurgist, some general pointers may be useful when selecting the material used for your tools. Basically, there are two main types of steel used to manufacture tools: stainless and carbon. These are not substantially different except that because chrome has been added to it, stainless steel is less likely to corrode than carbon steel. Having said that, the metal is stain-*less* not stain-*free*: if you really abuse it, it may well become tarnished.

Stainless steel has a reputation for being too hard to sharpen. This is more to do with the tempering of the steel than the nature of the metal itself. Historically, stainless steel has been the metal of choice for mass-produced knives, and many people in the modern world seem to have lost the ability to sharpen them. Thus, it makes sense to harden a knife edge so that it lasts. The downside is that when the blade does become dull, it is often badly damaged. This is because the more steel is hardened, the more brittle it becomes, making it more liable to break and lose a large chunk, in relative terms, of the blade. Furthermore, because of its excessive hardness, it is quite difficult to sharpen effectively, as sharpening involves grinding away metal to produce an edge.

There is probably a wider range of carbon-steel knives tempered to within workable tolerances than stainless-steel ones. The hardness of steel is measured on the Rockwell scale. With a working knife, you are looking to reach a compromise between the blade being hard enough to hold its edge, but not so hard that when it does become blunt, it is almost impossible to put that edge back on. Reputable knife manufacturers should be able to tell you the exact hardness of the tool's steel: look for something around the mid to high 50s on the Rockwell scale; any harder than this and it becomes increasingly frustrating and difficult to maintain the edge.

So, when choosing a knife, whether you buy stainless steel or carbon steel is very much a matter of personal taste. While carbon steel is more

Carbon steel (left) will rust more readily than stainless steel (right).

likely to rust, corrode or take on patina from the various activities that you are using it for, stainless steel – like a Hollywood celebrity who may have had 'work done' – is likely to stay shiny and lovely for much longer. On the one hand, if you spend a lot of time around coastal environments or are generally, like me, a bit rubbish at looking after your kit, you may opt for stainless steel; on the other hand, if you like the idea of your knife collecting memories of the work that it does, you may choose carbon steel. Do bear in mind that carbon will require a lot more maintenance and looking after than stainless.

Knives

I can't help thinking that I'm opening a huge can of worms by writing this section. Choosing the right knife has huge sections of the internet devoted to it, with arguments ranging far and wide across cyberspace and beyond as to the merits of this or that knife. Rather than become embroiled in that debate, I will just point out a few features to look for before you part with any of your hard-earned cash.

What I will say at the outset is that you don't need an armoury to practise any of the tasks described in this book – unless, of course, you're planning to become a deadly woodland assassin. In that case, you'll need several knives and axes – some of them of legendary proportions – and you'll have to think up suitably heroic names for your favourites: 'Bark Crusher', 'Sap Biter' and 'Oak's Bane' spring to mind.

Tangs

Back in the real world, having decided about the type of steel that you prefer, you are able to look at the many and various designs available on the market. At this point, it is worth familiarising yourself with the various tangs that are used in designing knives. The tang is the part of the knife that extends into the handle, and there are three main types to get to grips with (if you'll excuse the pun).

Full Tang

The strongest is a full tang, which extends all the way through the knife's handle with no narrowing or significant reduction in size. In fact, a full-tang knife handle consists of plates either screwed or riveted through the tang itself. Because there is no reduction in size, especially where the blade enters the handle, and no change in steel temper, these knives have the reputation of being almost unbreakable, if made correctly. On the downside they can be quite heavy, and it is difficult to find a mass-produced version, although more are becoming available now. However, you may find yourself limited to handmade tools, commanding handmade prices.

Needle or Nail Tang

The second strongest is a needle or nail tang. With this design, the tang extends all the way through the handle, but narrows significantly where the handle and blade meet. Where the tang exits from the handle, it is usually folded over and secured, often with a rivet. (It is common to find this set-up on billhooks as well.) The downside of this design is that the blade narrows significantly right at the point where there is often considerable sideways pressure.

I have also come across several designs where the tang is secured by heating it, and then pushing it through a pre-drilled hole in the handle: the tang burns its way through, ensuring a tight fit. However, this can create a weak point on the blade where it enters the handle, due, I believe, to the severe change in temper caused by having two parts of the knife exposed to extremely different temperatures.

On my courses, I have witnessed several quite expensive knives of this design snap at the handle. Therefore, I would purchase a knife with this sort of tang only if the handle is made from a variety of materials. Many Scandinavian knives have handles of antler bone, leather and wood that have been glued, rather than forced through using heat.

The prices and blade strength of knives vary considerably, depending on the type of tang.

n their simplicity, all these knives are well made and efficient.

Half or Partial Tang

The third-strongest tang is a half or partial tang. Usually, these are found in conjunction with a moulded plastic handle that has been sealed over the tang, often with inserts that match positions in the tang and hold it secure. In theory, this is the weakest arrangement, as there is less of the knife coming through the handle. On the plus side, there are lots of very cheap, high-quality knives available of this type.

I could go on and on about the merits of these various designs, but in reality, it doesn't matter which you choose, so long as it's fit for purpose and you like it. Price is obviously a huge factor: handmade, full-tang knives might cost hundreds of pounds, with partial-tang knives easily ten, even twenty times cheaper. What you should bear in mind is that it's very difficult to break any of these knives if they're made to a high standard, regardless of where the tang starts and stops.

If you are working a piece of wood with sufficient force that you feel you are putting your blade at risk, then perhaps you should consider making or using a different tool to ease the process. Normally, risks to the blade come from batoning firewood – in which case, making a wedge rather than banging on your knife (see Chapter 3 for more on batoning) might be the most appropriate course of action. If you have a knife with a ridiculously long blade, then certain sideways motions might damage it, but this is an unlikely scenario (unless you're stopping off to do a bit of carving on your way to an assassination!).

I have been using partial-tang knifes on courses for years and really, with the exception of one bad batch, the only time they break is when people hit the handle instead of the blade when batoning. I'm not sure why, but this design of knife really seems to object to this kind of treatment.

Axes

Many axes come with a convex bevel designed to maintain a robust edge, but for general use while camping and for basic carving, I favour a relatively lightweight axe with the blade ground to a flat bevel. The handle on mine is slightly longer than my forearm, which means that it is not too heavy to use when I'm carving, but I can still move my hands down the shaft to give me a reasonably effective tool for use with both hands. This is useful for splitting wood, and even for felling small trees. If I move my hand up to the head, effectively strangling it, I find that the long handle works like a little counterweight. It might be my imagination, but I find it less tiring to carve in this way, using the handle as a damper, in comparison to using a short-handled hatchet, even though the hatchet is likely to be lighter.

There are many great manufacturers of excellent axes out there, so it can be very difficult to choose one that really suits you. Again, price is an obvious factor, as is longevity, and you'll need to consider some of the other things that have already been mentioned, such as bevel angles. There are a few further aspects to be aware of when buying an axe.

Axe Handle
Start with the handle. Make sure that the shaft is straight grained and made of a quality hardwood. These days, shafts are mostly made from hickory, but in days gone by, British axe shafts were made from native ash. Straightness of the grain is important because if the axe takes excessive impact or, for whatever reason, energy is transferred back up the shaft, the shaft is less likely to break. This often happens when you are splitting wood and the axe head hasn't penetrated, perhaps due to hitting a hard

knot. In these circumstances, a shaft that doesn't have wood fibres running out at the sides is much more robust.

Axe Head

Next, look at the head of the axe, where the handle enters. You should try to find a shaft that doesn't narrow at all at this point. In practice, this means that the width of the shaft going into the eye of the axe is the same as its width when it comes out. Also, ensure that the head is securely connected, which means a reasonably thick, hardwood wedge that may be held in place with a metal staple.

For robustness, there should be a decent amount of metal around the eye. Generally, axes are tempered to be harder at the edge and softer towards the top. If the axe head was entirely hard-tempered, there is a danger that it will become too brittle and break due to shock or – as is often the case, in a bushcraft setting – when being used as a hammer to drive in stakes and suchlike.

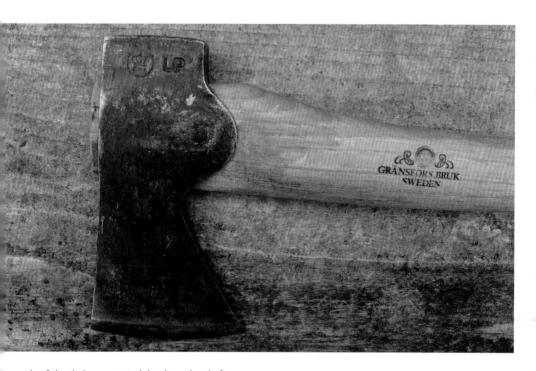

The grain of the timber runs straight along the shaft.

Axe Blade

Finally, it is a good idea to check that the bit, or blade, of the axe is in line with the shaft. Hold it up with the head closest to you, close one eye and look down the blade. Ensure that the line of the blade extends through to the very centre of the handle. A little bit of leeway in this alignment shouldn't be a problem, but if it's a long way off, it may affect performance in the way that it bites when striking.

In addition to my small axe, I have a larger one that has a full-length handle – by 'full-length', I mean approximately as long as my arm. I bought this axe for a trip into Arctic Sweden. My priority then was not craftwork but firewood, and the longer handle and slightly heavier head made this the ideal axe for the task (after all, at temperatures of –25°C, carving spoons may not be at the forefront of your mind!).

That said, it is possible to use an axe, even of this size and weight, one-handed for carving, although it is not particularly comfortable doing so.

I still find this axe very useful in the woods generally, and especially whenever I get a saw stuck: its bigger size makes getting the tool free a lot quicker. In fact, on occasion I have used it to free a trapped chainsaw.

Note the lack of narrowing of the metal, which forms a robust eye.

Splitting Maul

I also have a splitting maul for feeding the wood burner at home. This is slightly different to an axe, resembling nothing so much as a wedge on the end of a stick, but I much prefer it to an axe for splitting wood as it's very unlikely to get stuck in the rounds. I wouldn't spend a huge amount of money on a tool such as this, since it takes an absolute pounding, and tend to buy them with fibreglass or metal handles, as I lend them out to students. It's very likely that a beginner will miss the log that is to be split, and instead smash the shaft down just behind the head of the maul. Even the best-made wood shaft struggles to survive such treatment.

Saws

Compared with the vast array of knives that are available to the student of bushcraft and woodcraft, saws provide us with relatively few options. They are great tools to use in the outdoors; however, because (as already mentioned) you can learn to use them safely very quickly and they give very clean cuts, they make the sound pruning of trees and harvesting of materials possible.

In essence, we have three options for bushcraft: the bow saw, folding saw and pruning saw.

Bow Saw

We are doubtless all familiar with the bow saw. Although it is a little awkward and unwieldy for hiking about the woods, the bow saw comes into its own if you have a vehicle nearby, whether car or canoe.

There are two types of blades to be found on a bow saw: one is designed specifically for cutting green wood, while the other is for dry or seasoned wood. The differences between them are easy to spot: a green-wood blade will have four teeth splayed alternately out to either side of the blade, then every fifth one is a small V-shaped tooth called the 'raker', designed to clear sawdust from the cut or the 'kerf'. Due to the moisture in green wood, the sawdust becomes very spongy and sticky, so without this fifth tooth the blade would become jammed. Green-wood blades will also cut dry wood, but you will certainly notice the difference when trying to cut green wood with a dry-wood blade.

Note the raker tooth on this green-wood saw blade.

A true bow saw and a pruning saw.

Bearing this in mind, I would always pick a saw with a green-wood blade. It also may be worth selecting a saw with a frame that describes a true bow, since it could be operated at a pinch by two people.

Folding Saw

A slightly more portable option is the folding saw. These come in an array of different shapes and sizes, with not-insignificant differences in price. However, some are made from quite brittle materials and do tend to break, especially if they get jammed in the kerf.

It is better to go for a saw that offers more flexibility – bending before it breaks, which means that it can be flattened out again with the back of an axe. Such saws are slightly more expensive, but well worth the money. If you are going to spend money on a folding saw, pick one that locks in both the open and closed positions. These are much safer, especially when you need to reach into a tool bag or backpack to retrieve it.

Pruning Saw

Pruning saws are used by an increasing number of people for camping and woodcraft. Quality ones are much more expensive than bow saws or folding saws, but they cut extremely fast and effectively. They are also potentially much longer and therefore cumbersome to carry

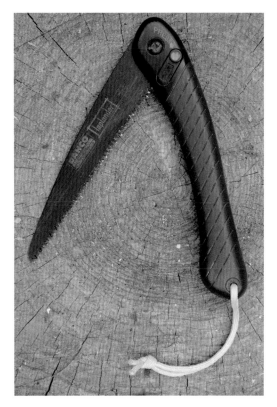

A folding saw.

around, certainly when compared with a folding saw. They have a curved blade, which can make it difficult to complete straight cuts, especially when making the back cut in felling and needing an even-thickness hinge.

Crook Knives, Draw Knives and Spoke Shaves

Crook Knife

The crook knife is a great little tool that comes with extreme variation in the radius of the hook at the end of the blade. The hooks range from very tight (ideal for hollowing out spoons and bowls) to relatively flat (which can be used not unlike a one-handed draw knife). These are extremely portable tools and very traditional, having their roots in several Native American woodworking practices.

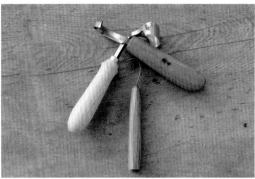

Crook knives.

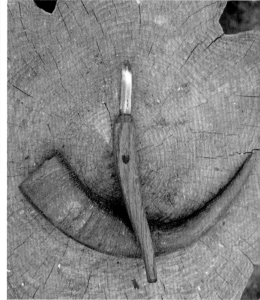

This variation of a crook knife can be used as a one-handed draw knife.

Draw Knife

The draw knives is a classic English woodworking tool: the only downside of using one is that it needs both hands. This implies that your workpiece must be clamped or held in some other way, which rather goes against the ethos of this book.

I have managed to brace bow staves between a stump and the pit of my stomach to operate draw knives and spoke shaves quite successfully, but this is hard to achieve with shorter workpieces. In addition, there is the obvious danger of falling on to the stave, and ritually disembowelling yourself. Cunningly, a safer alternative is to adapt a short piece of rope into a foot vice – this works quite well. (Please don't take this as a challenge – but with both crook knives and draw knives, it is quite difficult to cut yourself.)

It is possible to improvise a draw knife using a knotty stick and your normal knife. Simply cut a section of the stick around 10in (25cm) long with a knot at the end, drive the tip of your knife into the wood below this knot, and there is your draw knife. Be careful to ensure that the knife is secure and remember that the knot is important to stop the wood splitting completely.

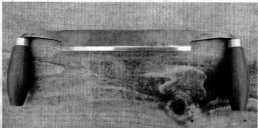

Clockwise from below: The blade of a draw knife; Using a knife as a draw knife, which requires two hands, by bracing it between the stomach and a log; Using a knotty stick to adapt a knife to function as a draw knife; A foot vice.

A selection of spoke shaves.

Spoke Shaves

Spoke shaves act a little like draw knives but control the depth at which the tool works. At a push, they can be used one-handed.

Other Useful Tools

There are a few further tools you might consider putting in your kitbag that would give you a few options, especially when finishing things finely, or when the grain of the wood is playing up and you're having trouble stopping chunks of wood lifting and ruining your best work.

Cabinet Scraper

I am very fond of the cabinet scraper, which consists of a square of sprung steel with a burr folded over the edge. This burr wears down with use and is maintained using a steel rod, such as a large screwdriver, and pressing it down at close to 90° to the scraper as you run it back and forth. The edge

ose-up of a scraper in use.

does the cutting; these tools take very fine shavings and don't tend to dig in. Bits of flint or even broken glass can serve as scrapers too.

Rasp

Rasps also work well, depending on their coarseness again, removing lots of little bits of material without digging in. These cannot be sharpened but do last for ages before they need replacing. I have had great success with farrier's rasps. Even though they were retired from their original task by the farrier as worn out, I find the ones that I have are still cutting bow staves for my students five years after having been discarded. Japanese saw rasps are exceptional pieces of kit, and well worth the money.

These tools can be used one-handed, so there is no need to clamp your work pieces.

(From top to bottom) Japanese saw rasp, farrier's rasp, normal wood rasp.

Maintenance

I will describe the process for sharpening a standard, flat, bevelled knife, but the method is essentially the same for all the tools I have discussed so far – except for saws, which generally (and perhaps unfortunately) are designed these days to be replaced rather than sharpened, and rasps.

The process for single-bevelled tools is practically the same as for crook knives, although slip stones or wet-and-dry sandpaper wrapped around a dowel may be easier to use when dealing with the radius. Convex bevels can be sharpened in the same way, but the tool will need to be rolled on the stone to maintain its profile.

Stones

Choice of stone can be difficult due to the huge range available. Just as with tools, what you end up with is usually a matter of personal preference, so bearing that in mind, I can only share my own thoughts and experiences, which you may choose to ignore completely. I am sure that arguments not unlike those about knives, although perhaps not quite so vehement, rage the length and breadth of the kingdom regarding the ultimate sharpening system.

Sharpening Stones at Home

If you become at all serious about working wood, then somewhere at home you may have two, possibly three grades of stone: for the sake of convenience, let us call them coarse, medium and fine. These will be bench stones, which are generally quite large and, in some cases, quite heavy. It is not practical to attempt to carry these in a backpack, so for a more mobile sharpening system you will have to think again, and I will offer a few thoughts on the subject below.

The home system allows you to establish a good edge quickly and accurately, as opposed to trying to sharpen your best axe with a 3in (7.5cm) travelling stone – not impossible, but also not especially convenient, in fact, rather tedious! The coarse stone allows you to remove material very quickly, which is great if your knife is badly damaged; of course, being the hardened and honed woodsmen and women that you are, you would never let your knife get into such a condition. However, it may be worth having one in your collection, together with a flat file, just in case any less well-informed acquaintances need your help.

Japanese Waterstones

I most like to use Japanese waterstones. They are fast-cutting and are clean as they work with water instead of oil. They come in specific measured grades, so it's much easier to distinguish the coarse from the fine. I have an 800-grit, 1,200-grit and 5,000-grit. To be honest, the 5,000-grit is seldom used; I find a strop, together with honing paste, does the same job and the superfine stones are very soft and fragile, so it's easy to take big chunks out of them while sharpening.

Anyway, these waterstones are incredibly easy to use: immerse them in a bath until they stop fizzing and they are ready to go. (When I say bath, by the way, I don't mean *the* bath – any suitably sized, water-holding vessel will do.)

Waterstones do need to be kept wet as they are used, and they should be flattened after you have finished each time. This is to prevent them becoming dished, which they inevitably will unless you take care of them, especially when repeatedly sharpening the same type of tool. You can prevent dishing either by using one of the special flattening stones that can be bought, or simply rubbing one stone against another.

The Strop

Another key ingredient in the sharpening process is the strop. This might be a purpose-cut piece of leather tacked onto a board, or just your belt. Strops can be made from anything relatively smooth: a piece of wood, or the birch polypore fungus, too.

In essence, the strop is there to make the edge more robust by removing fragments of metal left behind by the main sharpening. These fragments are an inevitable by-product of wearing away the working edge of your cutting tool. Imagine working the bevel on both sides of your knife. Eventually the edge will become so fine that no amount of sharpening can make that edge any finer; when this happens, the tool starts to produce what is known as a 'wire edge'. Carrying on with the same grade of stone will not make the tool's edge any sharper. Each grade can only cut so many microns of metal before a finer grade is required, and all that happens if you continue is that more of the knife is worn away and wasted, without it getting any sharper. This formation of a wire edge happens throughout the various grades of stone. It is finally removed by using a strop.

Travelling Stones

If you like the idea of disappearing into the woods for a few days and doing some woodwork, you may wish to take a micro-sharpening system with you. These come in many forms, from purpose-built travelling stones to homemade versions of the same. I would urge you to put your travels into perspective: for a normal camping trip, during which you might wish to take on some of the green woodworking projects in this book, it is unlikely that you will need a full-scale sharpening system. In fact, for general camping it is unlikely you would need to sharpen your knife at all, unless you're out for a very long period. At the most basic level, you could consider carrying a small amount of honing paste, which is slightly abrasive and could be used in conjunction with your belt. This would enable you to keep your blade edge topped up.

In truth, I'm not a big fan of purpose-built travelling stones: they are generally quite small and don't allow proper sharpening. This is because, when laid flat, there is generally not enough clearance for the knife handle to allow them to be used like a bench system. I much prefer taller travel stones that, at a push, can be used in the hand, but also allow for a good amount of pressure to be applied when they are placed on a natural bench, such as a stump. Aside from the size, all the other considerations described above apply to a portable system.

Travelling stones.

Sharpening Your Tools

Before describing the sharpening process in detail, I should explain exactly what sharpening is. The obvious answer is, of course, the process of making a tool sharp (I'll be describing the method for knives here). However, that begs the question of what 'sharp' means. Removing the damage that results in a dull edge is part of it, but so is maintaining a bevel angle, a bevel profile (for example, convex or flat), and ensuring that the shoulder or part of the blade where the edge starts is set at a consistent distance throughout its length. Finally, the knife should be stropped to remove any remnant of the wire edge, making the blade as robust as possible.

Sharpening Technique

- Assuming that waterstones are being used, first make sure that they are wet, and that throughout the process they remain so.

- Lay the knife blade on the stone and tilt it forward, until all the bevel is in contact with the stone.

- Apply pressure as you push the knife away, doing your best to maintain contact with the stone along the full length of the blade. This can be achieved by sweeping the knife left or right, depending on your handedness.

- Alternatively, you can work different parts of the blade at different times. I tend to work the area closest to the handle, then move out to get the rest of the blade and the tip. The sweep of the blade towards the tip is particularly difficult to keep in contact with the stone: it might be necessary to raise the handle slightly to do so.

- It is possible to do all of this in one motion, sliding the knife to the side and raising the handle at the same time, but it's quite tricky to master the technique, and not entirely necessary.

Wire Edge Problems

When I first learnt to sharpen, I was taught to use this technique and make six strokes on one side of the blade, before turning it over and making six strokes on the other. The second set of strokes is most conveniently made by reversing the blade and bringing it back towards you.

This traditional method works well, but when a person is new to sharpening knives, it can be very difficult to know when to stop – when sharpness has been achieved. This is due to our old friend the wire edge, which – as we have already discussed – appears when a stone has cut the blade as fine as it possibly can. The wire edge is a great indication of when you have gone far enough; the problem with the traditional method is that the wire edge is constantly knocked off, making it tricky to know when to stop.

It is much easier just to work one side of the knife until the wire edge forms. It appears as a lip or a snag, which can be felt with the fingers. It forms on the uppermost side of the tool, and once it has appeared along the whole length of the blade, switch the knife over and work the other side until you have raised a second wire edge. This process can be repeated through various grades of stone: in other words, work both edges on the coarse stone, both edges on the medium stone, and finally perhaps, both edges on the fine stone, depending on how thorough you wish to be.

Personally, I feel that stopping at the medium grade or 1,200 Japanese waterstone is more than enough. The last thing I do is to gently work the edges, so that no wire can be felt. When this has been achieved, any remnant of wire edge – which by now will be so tiny as not to be felt – can be knocked off using a strop.

As mentioned previously, stropping is important, as any wire left after sharpening will break off when the knife is used – often taking a piece of the blade with it – which blunts your knife. When stropping, be sure to work the blade on both sides by dragging it: this avoids cutting your strop and ensures that the wire edge is removed from both sides.

Periodic stropping can also be used to delay the need for a full-blown sharpening session. Often, the knife may appear blunt due to the edge having become, in effect, folded over. Stropping the knife thoroughly can often 'stand' the edge up and make the tool serviceable again.

* * *

1. Lay the blade flat on the stone.
2. Tilt it forward on to the bevel blade flat on the stone.
3. Work one edge at a time.
4. Raise the knife handle to work the tip of the blade.
5. When stropping, drag the blade.
6. To test your knife is sharp, cut through a piece of paper.

Those are pretty much all the basics you need for sharpening, but do remember: throughout the process, the blade should be checked to ensure that the bevel angle and profile are maintained. It is easy to see how the metal is being worn away, and to correct yourself from pushing the knife too far forward or laying it too far back, thereby changing the bevel angle. Just keep checking which areas are becoming polished by your actions.

Once you have your knife sharp, test it using a sheet of paper: the knife should slice cleanly through it without snagging.

3

Using Tools and Carving

I have been carving small objects for many years now, especially on my courses. The majority are spoons, as carving a spoon is a great project that doesn't take too long but it teaches pretty much all the major knife techniques. Even better, all being well at the end of the learning process, the student has a nice, functional object to take home.

The problem I have as a teacher, though, is that demonstrating spoons on a regular basis leads to lots of these implements being produced. When I met my now wife, I started to bring these artefacts home as love tokens. Finished to a high order, with all the sentiment I could muster, I was very proud of my creations. Unfortunately, after receiving six or seven spoons, any potential life partner will start to look at you a little oddly. No doubt, leaving wooden spoons about the place – in the car, under the pillow, next to the kettle and so on – starts to wear thin. With the benefit of hindsight, I can imagine it might make a person feel a little uncomfortable – certainly in the early stages of a relationship – rather like a cat owner who finds a mouse on the doorstep and is left wondering where the next 'gift' will turn up.

After a long chat (and some counselling), I got over this stage – and made her a bow instead.

Carved spoons.

It is worth pointing out at this juncture that it is not my intention to cover the whole array of techniques available to the green woodworker. There are already several great books that delve deeper into traditional woodland crafts than I intend to go in this book (see the Further Reading section). Instead, my focus here is on exploring possibilities for the student of bushcraft and wilderness skills, and the tools most likely to be available to them outdoors, or to anyone who, like me, can't afford or be bothered with assembling a huge workshop full of kit when all they want to do is mess around with some bits of wood.

Using Tools Safely

When it comes to safety, there are a few general principles that apply equally across the range of sharp tools with which we are likely to find ourselves out in the woods. There are also a handful of principles that relate to specific tools – we will deal with these as we describe various processes and techniques.

Watching Yourself

First, take a little time to think about all the accidents that could possibly happen when you are wielding your favourite bladed tool. These will range from severed limbs and run-ins with axes, to the gentle nick sustained when unsheathing your knife. It is important to consider the worst and most likely problems that you will face.

I would venture to suggest that the arterial cut is one of the more disappointing accidents that can occur, with a slice through the femoral artery really likely to put a dampener on your day. Because of the vessel's size, a cut to the femoral artery is particularly dangerous: it can cause a person to bleed out in a matter of minutes. Cunningly, most of the arteries that are easiest to get at are on the inside of the body: the femoral is on the inner side of the legs, the brachial on the inner side of the arms.

Imagine humans as creatures running around on all fours (which is surprisingly easy and fun to do with some people). In this scenario, the arteries are all protected on the inside of the body, along with our internal organs. However, standing upright and marching around like we own the planet exposes all the soft and leaky bits to anything the world throws at them.

When using a knife, if we adopt a position that ensures our vulnerable areas are protected from the blade, first, by the workpiece, and second, by the muscle and bone on the outside of the body, we have a very good chance of avoiding cutting ourselves at all, and certainly avoiding a major bleed. In practice, protecting yourself in this way requires carving on the outer edges of the body, or if you are sitting down, leaning forward so that the elbows rest on the knees, thereby avoiding the inner thighs and that infamous femoral artery.

The third major artery easily available for puncture is the carotid, located in the neck. If anyone really is careless enough to be carving close to this area, it is probably natural selection kicking in. Perhaps we should not interfere with these complex biological processes and allow people to leave the gene pool unmolested.

Slightly less serious, but more common injuries that occur with edged tools are deep, penetrating wounds. These should always be looked at by professionals, as they have the potential to damage or completely sever tendons. If you suspect that you have damaged a tendon, go straight to Accident & Emergency at the nearest hospital. Resist the temptation to start wiggling digits to check whether you are still attached, as a partially cut tendon can be easily snapped by such actions. When tendons are cut, they begin to retreat up the arm, which can be quite a problem for the surgeon who has to locate them and stitch them back together. While a partially severed tendon is not ideal, it is still a far easier prospect to deal with than one that is hurrying back up to your armpit.

Fortunately, it is simple to avoid these types of injuries.

! Never have the hand that is not holding the knife below the tool.

In fact, many injuries can be avoided just by leaving the workpiece longer than is strictly necessary (it always can be shortened at the last minute). By doing this, there is no need to have the spare hand anywhere near a carving tool.

These are incorrect work positions and endanger the inside of your legs and the femoral artery.

Watching Others

You should spare a thought for other people's soft and squidgy bits. I recommend staying at approximately 10ft (3m) away from the nearest person when carving with a knife, and a little further for general axe work. In my opinion, people directly behind and in front of a person who is throwing an axe are in most danger. Should that person lose control, or more likely lose their grip, there is no real limit to the distance that their tool may travel. So, while sensible distances should be left either side of the worker, I suggest that nobody stand behind or in front of a person using an axe, at the very least when they're undertaking heavy work. When carving with an axe, the safe working distance is similar to that for knife work.

Nonetheless, when working with any bladed tool, it is wise to carry a first aid kit. Depending on the nature of the tools being used, your first aid kit might range from plasters and small dressings, right up to large wound dressings and even clotting agents, when you are out working with an axe.

Using a Knife

(Techniques for using a knife safely are illustrated in the spoon-carving sequence below.)

 l of these techniques are possible without having to se a big, heavy block. (Note the fist grip.)

The knife doesn't change its plane of motion.

When you are carving, it is very useful to have a block onto which you can cut down with both axe and knife. This means that you don't bury your work, especially so when you're splitting wood, and it stops you stuffing your razor-sharp blade into the ground. Contrary to one tale I was told (no doubt originating from old wives), inserting a blade into the earth will not sharpen it and can only dull the edge.

Using a backstop will give you confidence when making bold and powerful cuts. If you not only have a block, but also have a choice as to how big it is, get one that allows comfortable movement without you having to bend over too far: a log that is too small for your height will give you a bad back.

If you can't find a block, all of the work considerations described below can be met by kneeling down and cutting onto a board, split log or old fallen tree. Furthermore, these techniques work with the minimum of equipment.

Try to ensure that your tool never changes direction as you carve, by which I mean that it should move in the same plane with each stroke. If you wish to change angles, move the workpiece, not the knife. This applies to any of the grips described here. In my experience, people often get cut when their knife is forced into a strange angle. Instead, imagine the knife going up and down like a guillotine, with the workpiece moving when new angles are required.

Batoning

Batoning with a knife is the technique of striking the back of the blade with a heavy log or mallet – or at least one heavy enough to push the blade through the chosen piece of wood. It is especially useful for splitting deadwood – often when preparing firewood – but it is also a useful technique for crosscutting green wood.

When splitting wood vertically, as you might do to obtain firewood or feather sticks, imagine the workpiece and your knife as the apex of a triangle, with your feet forming the other two points. Hold your knife at 90° to your body. This means that not only can you see what you're hitting and are presenting yourself with a broad target, but also should things go horribly wrong, the knife tends to roll away from you to the side.

Place the wood that you are going to split on the far side of the block and take your triangular stance.

Bury the blade of your knife in the wood.

Push on the handle and hit the blade. If the knife works itself out, don't be afraid to bang it down again.

4. If the knife gets stuck, gently tap it out.

5. If the wood is too tough, you might need to use a wedge.

6. You should end up with two equal pieces.

- Hold the knife in your weaker hand, and the baton in your stronger one.

- Lay the knife across the diameter of the log, with its handle as close to the wood as possible. This ensures that once the tool enters the wood, there is enough blade sticking out to act as a target for your baton. If the knife is not inserted up to the hilt, there is a chance that the blade will flex and break or pop out of its handle.

- Position the knife in such a way that you split the wood into even halves, otherwise there is a danger that the split will run off to the side where there is less material.

! Whether you are using an axe or a knife, get into the habit of placing the wood that you are splitting at the far side of your chopping block. This is especially important with an axe, since it means that any missed strokes will hit the block first before the axe careers off – potentially towards you.

The process used to split the workpiece is to push down on the handle and strike the tip of the knife, gradually working it through the wood. The initial split is always the hardest since the fibres in the wood are more difficult to break apart at first. However, as wood dries faster on the outside that the inside, there is often a drying crack in the end grain, which can assist your splitting greatly – use these cracks whenever possible.

Before any of this happens, first carve yourself a wedge. This helps you deal with the eventuality of your knife becoming stuck. It also can help you to split a stubborn piece of wood without putting additional strain on your knife. To carve the wedge, use the fist grip (see below) and block.

Stop Cuts
Batoning can be adapted with the use of stop cuts. These are especially useful if you think there is a danger that the split you are creating will run into the spoon, bow or object you are trying to carve out. A series of stop cuts will create a weak place that the split will gravitate towards.

our wedge should have a long taper to enter the wood, with the edges knocked off for robustness and a bevel edge where it will be hit to resist splitting.

Chiselling

A further adaptation of batoning uses the knife a little like a chisel. Hold your knife against the workpiece with your thumb, then hit the blade with the baton. Changing the angle of the knife using this technique will give you a lot of options for the controlled removal of wood.

Chiselling and the use of stop cuts.

Crosscutting Green Wood

If you are crosscutting green wood, imagine the fibres within the stick as bundles of spaghetti running the length of the material. If you approach these bundles with a blade at 90°, you will be trying to sever all the fibres at once. It is much more efficient to cant the blade slightly, to sever the fibres at an angle. (This knowledge can be applied to crosscutting with other tools, including axes and billhooks – in fact, it is useful to think of slicing at an angle for all carving techniques.)

To baton at an angle, you will have to overhang your chopping block, allowing the handle of the knife to come down into space; otherwise, beating on the blade of the knife only bangs the handle against your block.

1. Hold your knife at a slight angle.

2. It may take several hits to sever the fibres.

3. Severing the fibres with this technique is effortless.

Rosette or Rose Cuts

This cut is an alternative crosscutting technique. In essence, it involves making several shallow cuts around the circumference of a rod. This sequence of cuts can be repeated several times, if necessary, until it is possible to break the wood easily. One half of the timber is left resembling a flower head, while the other half has a gentle point. Not only does this approach require less energy than other crosscutting methods, but it can be used to begin creating a point. The rosette or rose cut also can be made with heavier tools such as axes and billhooks, with or without a baton.

Freeing a Stuck Knife

The Wedge

As with any tool, if you use a knife for long enough when splitting or batoning timber, eventually you will get it stuck. This is where the wedge really comes into its own.

Place the wedge directly behind the blade and gently tap it home with your baton. Don't worry about the knife falling – obviously, collect it if you can when it comes loose to put in its sheath – but if it falls free, *do not try to catch it*. In any case, the wedge should be gently tapped home, either freeing the knife or breaking the wood in half, whichever comes first.

If for any reason you have neglected to make a wedge, you can gently tap the handle vertically up and down, backwards and forwards, until the knife comes free.

! Do not be tempted to grab hold of the work with one hand and your knife with the other, then try to rock the knife free. I once saw a piece of wood open during this process, and the person holding it completely sever two tendons in his hand.

Grips and Other Carving Techniques

The Fist Grip

Perhaps the simplest, most powerful and, in many ways, safest knife grip comes from holding the tool in your fist. When practising this grip, do not be tempted to put your thumb on the back of the blade. This does not give you more control, it only increases the chances of you getting a sore thumb.

1. Removing branches is always easiest if you work from bottom to top.
2. Push on the knife handle to make an angle cut.
3. Rotate the stick and repeat several times.
4. Rock the stick to break it.
5. One side of the break should now resemble a flower.

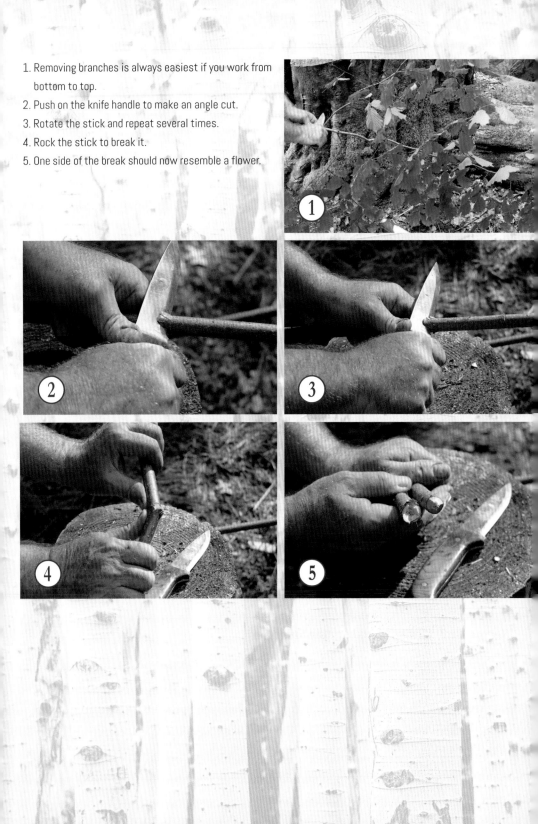

When used in conjunction with a chopping block, the fist grip is a very comfortable and safe position to adopt. The knife should be on the same side of the body as the hand holding it: if you're right-handed, the knife would be close to your right leg, with the workpiece held by your left hand. The arm holding the workpiece crosses the body and is braced against the stump, which means that the vulnerable femoral arteries are protected, first by the workpiece, and second by the muscle and bone on the outside of the leg. The arm is fairly straight, working up and down like a machine, which makes the technique very efficient, with the weight evenly distributed over the cutting edge. Slightly overhang the block with the knife, so you don't smash your knuckles on the down stroke.

Another advantage of this stance is that if your arms become tired, you can partially lock your knife arm, allowing your weight to come down on the workpiece by bending your knees. With the work close to your body, you will be able to work for longer since this is much less tiring than trying to cut at arm's length.

The Chest Lever

Using the chest lever technique.

Sometimes also referred to as 'chicken wings', this technique can help you take a rest when carving for long periods, as it uses a different set of muscles. Start by holding the knife in the fist grip, then reverse the knife so that the blade is pointing towards your elbow. The workpiece is held in your weaker hand, and the carving takes place by opening the chest. A variation on this, using the same technique but lower down on the body, can be employed.

Bracing

A further variation on the fist grip is to brace your knife against a small tree, your knee, or indeed any appropriate vertical object that you can find around the camp. If using your knee, make sure that the knife is braced on the outer leg. Holding your knife close to the base of its handle, brace part of the handle or even the blade against your knee. The workpiece is then dragged against it, while your knife stays static. You should put the knife on the same side as your dominant hand.

The knife must be on the outside of the body, otherwise there is a real danger that as you pull the workpiece towards your crotch, you might sustain an embarrassing and (especially for men) painful injury. Also, if you happen to slip and inadvertently close your legs, releasing the knife, it is much less likely to stab you.

Reinforced Grips

Reinforced grips are some of my favourites, as they give you great power at the same time as great control. However, they can be difficult techniques to describe, and there are variations.

Here's one to start you off. For this grip, once again the knife is held in the traditional fist grip and then reversed, so that the blade faces the elbow. Use two or three fingers on the non-knife-wielding hand to push on the back of the blade, leaving your thumb and forefinger of the same hand to hold the workpiece. This technique looks more dangerous than it is: you are not actually carving towards yourself. It is twisting the wrist that gives the technique its power and control, which stops the blade coming anywhere near the body.

When you brace using the body, ensure the knife is on the outside of your body.

This stance is incorrect and puts you at risk from the knife and the workpiece.

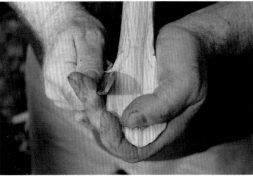

Clockwise from left: Great power and control can be achieved when using a reinforced grip; Help yourself when carving by pushing with the other hand; Strangling the knife.

A similar principle underpins a second technique: using the traditional fist grip but carving away from you. This time, use the thumb of your weaker hand to push on the back of the blade – in fact, it is much easier and less painful to hold the knife slightly down the handle, and use your thumb against the handle rather than the blade.

Reinforced grips can be adapted by moving your hand up the blade, effectively strangling it. Very fine work can be done this way, using the very tip of the blade and the shallow cutting radius that it creates. You may even find that the reinforcing push of the non-working hand isn't needed.

Using a Saw

Describing the safe use of the saw is apt to be a brief section of this book since, in practice, it is a very simple tool to use. Regardless of the type of saw, the technique is always the same.

Should a saw decide to jump out of the cut when you are sawing a piece of wood, ninety-nine times out of 100 it will jump to the inside of your body. If your spare hand is next to the blade, invariably it will damage that hand. To avoid this happening, simply reach over the blade – or through it, depending on the type of saw being used. Should the blade now bounce out, it will only make contact with the underside of your arm, and then only with the non-pointy bits of the saw.

Freeing a Stuck Saw

Should the saw become stuck, it is usually because you have misjudged the tension and compression in the timber to be cut. The tension side of timber is the area that will cause the cut to open, falling away from the saw. The compression side is the area that causes the cut to close in on itself, thus trapping the saw.

avoid injury, simply pass your hand through or over the saw.

Depending on where the tension lies, it may be necessary to raise up or push down on the timber to cause the compression side to open up. Of course, judging which side is most likely to close on the saw before beginning work is the real answer here. Generally, a log that is supported free of the ground at both ends will have the compression wood at the top; conversely, a log supported only at one end, with the area to be cut in free space, will have the compression wood underneath.

Using an Axe

How to Throw an Axe

'Throwing an axe' is actually rather a good description of what you have to do. Like many things, there are a couple of tips and tricks that make the process more efficient. Once again, I'll describe the process for a right-handed person.

! Before you start slinging your axe about the woods, please ensure that there is nothing in the vicinity that might catch its head or shaft. Low branches are particularly dangerous.

Now, we're ready to chop some wood:

- Your left hand should be somewhere near the bottom of the axe shaft, the right under the head, to carry it upwards. This is very important if you're using a heavy tool – a large splitting maul, for example – as it is almost impossible (as well as painful) to try to lift it from the end of the handle alone.

- The right hand takes the head over the right shoulder. There is no need to bring the tool directly over your head: as well as it being more effort than is needed, it could be dangerous. Instead, as the axe travels down, bring its head in line with the centre of the body.

1. Put the wood on the far side of your chopping block and carry the axe head.

2. Slide the hand down the shaft as the axe is thrown.

3. Slightly bending the knees adds power to the axe stroke.

Right: Sometimes it is safer to use a baton when making firewood with an axe.

- Your right hand effectively throws the axe head away, while simultaneously sliding down the shaft to join the left.

- Bending the knees at the point of impact can add greatly to the force behind the blow. It also saves the lower back from strain since it encourages the spine to stay straight.

If you are tired, injured or for some other reason unable to throw the axe safely and accurately, you can baton the axe head through a piece of wood to split it. This is often a safer technique, particularly after a long day in the woods, when all you want to do is get your fire going with a minimum of fuss (and obviously, the minimum of axe-related wounds).

Kneeling is often the most effective and safest approach when chopping wood with an axe.

Considerations When Splitting Wood

When working on a round or backstop, place the log to be split at the far side of that stump. If you miss the piece of wood that you are aiming at, your axe should bury itself safely into the backstop. Also, hold the axe as far away from your body as is practical, but avoid overextending your arms and locking out your elbows, as this may lead to injury.

Have a dry run. Using a short-handled hatchet, you'll notice that your body and in particular your legs are still close enough to be hit should the axe glance off the backstop. This is where kneeling down comes in. If you try this for your dry run, you should find that even with a short handle, it is nearly impossible to hit yourself before the axe becomes buried in the ground. When using a stump, don't be embarrassed if you have to adjust its height.

Your dry run should also include a slow swing of the axe through the arc that you intend to use. This will confirm that you aren't going to catch the tool on any surrounding branches or vegetation.

- Try to position your feet in a straight line, with the axe head and workpiece forming the tip of the triangle for which your legs serve as a base. Should one of your legs be significantly further forward than the other, there is a big chance of injury, should the axe glance off.

- *It is extremely important to be safe around other people.* The worst accidents that could happen to somebody else are likely to result from you losing control of your axe, especially if it escapes your grip.

- *Nobody should be alongside you, but I recommend that nobody stands directly behind you or in front of you for several yards* – perhaps even tens of yards. It's amazing how far you can throw these tools, either by design or accident – think Olympic hammer thrower, if you're in any doubt.

- *Always have a large wound dressing handy when using an edge tool.* Should things go wrong, the damage inflicted by an axe, in particular, is quite impressive.

Freeing a Stuck Axe

If you split enough wood, it is inevitable that at some point you'll get your axe stuck. Probably the worst thing you could do when trying to free it is wiggle the handle from side to side. (I remember doing this once as a child, with an axe borrowed from the local scout troop: I snapped the shaft just behind the head. As you may imagine, I wasn't very popular – especially as I wasn't even in the scouts.)

You may be able to free a stuck axe by tapping on the end of the handle, up and down, to gradually work the tool out of the wood. Alternatively, if you can do so without strain, it is possible to pick the whole thing up and slam the axe down on the backstop, with the stuck log uppermost. Often, this both frees the axe and splits the wood. Don't make a Herculean effort to lift something that is too big for you: in the woods, always remind yourself where your intestines belong.

Many years ago, I was splitting wood in a farmer's field – this was before the days of mobile phones – when I got my axe stuck. With due attention to safety, I began to tap the axe up and down at the end of the handle to free the blade. My other hand was quite close to the head of the axe. When the axe came free, it caused the split in the wood suddenly to close up.

Using the block to free a trapped axe.

Unfortunately, it closed on a large chunk of flesh at the base of my thumb and trapped it. This was quite embarrassing, as I was standing alone in a field with no means of contacting anybody. Having a round of wood, perhaps 18in (45cm) in diameter and 8in (20cm) thick, stuck to my hand, I surmised, would make driving for help problematic. Eventually I did manage to free myself, but only with the loss of a good deal of skin. The moral of the story is: keep your hand clear when freeing your axe.

Splitting Firewood

One of the easiest and simplest ways to get used to using your axe is to chop firewood. It's a perfect opportunity to put into practice all the techniques that we have been talking about – throwing the axe, freeing a stuck axe and ensuring that your stance is correct.

It's worth considering which type of material to start with: for any piece of wood, the cleaner it is, the easier the split will be. By clean, I mean free from knots, twists, bends and any other defects. A gnarly lump of elm, for example, would be better left for the habitat pile or to serve as an all-night burning log, depending on the size of your wood burner.

Once you've broken your log down into small enough elements, you can practise making kindling:

- Hold the shaft of your axe at the end with your stronger hand, and a stick of firewood, also at the end, with your weaker hand, and bang them both sharply down onto your chopping block.

- With small-diameter wood such as this, if you get the axe stuck just give it a gentle twist: invariably, this will split the wood.

It is also possible to split quite large lumps of wood without using a chopping block, but care must be taken to avoid smacking the axe into your shin or swinging it too vigorously and embedding the axe head in your lower back.

Move your axe and the wood in conjunction with each other to make firewood.

Body position and using a short, snappy motion are crucial here.

- Place the wood you want to split on a small round of wood, with one end slightly raised and the other touching the ground. This ensures that the head of your axe is in no danger of hitting the ground.

- Straddle your legs, a bit like doing the splits (depending on the length of your axe shaft, you might have to be quite supple to achieve this manoeuvre). The idea is to place your heels at least level with but preferably slightly ahead of the point where the axe will strike.

- Deliver a sharp blow to the end grain of the timber that is to be split, but make sure you pull the blow: if you follow through, you are quite likely to swing underneath and through your legs, risking injury to your back. This requires a really snappy movement.

! One final thought: under no circumstances tie an axe to your body, certainly not by using a wrist loop.

These loops are only intended for hanging up the tool. I was laying hedges one winter, many years ago, and dropped a billhook that was tied to me in this way. It swung sharply in towards my thigh, cutting my leg quite badly. Remember: I cut myself so that you don't have to!

Carving With an Axe
Much of what I've said about keeping safe with a knife applies equally to using the axe. Work on a block whenever possible and try to protect the insides of your legs from the blade, using both the workpiece and the muscle and bone of the outside of your body.

Carving effectively does take a bit of practice. You need to learn the correct angle for removing wood quickly, safely and accurately, especially when using a double-bevel axe. As with knife-carving, think about moving the work and not the axe, which should be moving up and down in the same consistent plane. The work can be tilted over, should the angle need to be changed.

1. Using the axe close to the head, with the handle acting as a comfortable counterweight.

2. Making a series of stop cuts, and then cutting them all off, is very effective.

3. The weight of the axe can be used like a plane.

4. Step back and hold the axe closer to the end of the shaft power blows. Note the position of the non-working hand

5. Always change the angle of the piece of wood, not your tool.

6. Making wooden wedges, or 'gluts', is great axe-carving practice.

To remove wood quickly with an axe, it is often most effective to make short stop cuts all the way up the work, then these can be knocked off with a single blow. Stop cuts also can be made with a saw for small craft items such as spoons, as well as to remove large amounts of material quickly for projects such as bow-making. Material then can be knocked off using an axe or knife, perhaps with a baton.

With all edge tools, little and often is the best method for removing wood quickly, rather than using large, violent swings. Swinging big can be dangerous, is often ineffective, and ultimately may lead to you to ruining the workpiece. Once again, carving on a stump or some other form of backstop can be the most effective way of keeping in control and saving the edge of your tool from damage.

Crosscutting With an Axe

Crosscutting is, to my mind, the most dangerous activity that you can take on with an axe. Not only is the tool travelling towards you, but it is likely to be doing so at an angle directly in line with your shin. However, the task can be carried out relatively safely if you follow a few basic rules:

- Make sure that when the head of the axe hits the wood, it is parallel to the ground and nowhere near the top of the log. As you're cutting and removing wood, a slight overhang or shelf of uncut timber is produced if you are doing it right. It may be necessary to prop up the wood somehow, to give enough clearance. You also may want to consider pegging lengths of wood to stop them rolling around.

- Your feet should be wide apart – how wide will depend on the length of the axe handle that you are using. They should definitely be behind the log, and therefore protected from the axe. This technique involves the axe entering the wood on its side.

Once again, you may find it easier and safer to kneel – in which case, the axe enters the wood on the top. However, there is more risk of sticking the axe into the ground when you kneel. It also means that you can't work from both sides of the timber, which may make it difficult to chop through, especially if you are unable to roll the log to reach the other side.

When crosscutting, think of the axe as a splitting rather than a cutting tool. Too many people fall into the trap of pounding relentlessly on the log, getting nowhere and concluding that it would be quicker and easier to saw the thing in half.

- Start by making a shallow 'V' cut at roughly 45°.

- Make a second 'V' cut a couple of inches (5cm) away. You have effectively created a pair of stop cuts with a piece of uncut wood in the middle.

- Then – hopefully with a single blow – break the chip in-between the two cuts, splitting it down the grain.

- Repeat this double cut on the other side of the first broken-out chip. You should now have a piece of uncut wood between these two areas, which in turn can be broken out.

This process can be repeated all the way through the log. If done correctly, this technique makes axe work relatively effortless. Since the axe – or at least the weight of the axe – is doing most of the work, you shouldn't find yourself battering your log and making no progress.

The problem arises when you lose sight of the fact that you're creating chips to break out. If you start merely hitting the log, the blade continually gravitates towards the apex of the triangle you have created. This achieves little apart from getting you worn out, tired and fed up.

With a big log, continue this splitting-out process past halfway, then don't be afraid to roll it over and begin again from the other side. With a very big log you may have to roll it again, ending up approaching it from three or even four sides before you can break it in half. Be sensible, though: when you get very close to coming through the other side of the log, try to break it manually rather than using your axe.

! It is at these moments, when nearly through the wood, that you are likely to strike too hard and put the axe into your shin.

. Make two notches, a few inches apart.

. Break out the wood between them.

–4. Repeat this process until you are just past halfway, then cut from the other side. Keep your feet protected, neeling down if necessary, and if you don't create a shelf, you are cutting too close to the top of the log.

When a crosscut has been made to perfection, the size of the opening of its 'V' will match the diameter of the log being worked on. Any wider than this and wood has been wasted; any narrower and the head of the axe will not be able to reach the point of the 'V'.

A similar technique is used when making sink cuts and back cuts with an axe. The only difference is that one edge is kept flat (Chapter 1 has more information on these felling cuts).

Cleaving

Imagine you have felled a tree – a beautiful, clean, straight length of ash, for example. You crosscut a nice length of wood, perhaps 6ft (1.8m) long or more. You now need to split it into halves, quarters or perhaps even further, depending on the diameter of the stick you are working on, from which you plan to make the perfect longbow. The description of splitting that follows is appropriate for all diameters of timber and, within reason, all lengths. You can scale down this technique to work with knives and small wedges, or scale it right up for heavy timber gateposts and post-and-rail fencing. Any splitting, carving or making projects using wood are so much easier if the timber chosen is clean – in fact, some projects demand it. (As mentioned previously, in woodcraft terms, 'clean' means free of defects).

To get your head around the complexities of cleaving, it is useful to start with material with a very small diameter. Clean, straight, hazel rods, which at their thickest point are the same diameter as the base of your thumb, are great for this.

! Remember: always to try to split with equal amounts of wood on either side of the blade.

If you don't do this, the split is very likely to run off to the side, where there is least material. In practice, this usually means splitting directly in half, then quarters and eighths and so on, until the required size of material is reached. With smaller-diameter material, it is possible to correct the split if it does run off simply by pushing on the fattest side.

- To begin, cut into the wood at its end with your blade: this is most easily done on a block. (I always start at the thinnest end, since this gives me increasing material if I need to correct any run-off.)

- Grasping the rod between your knees, with its end on the block, hold the knife vertically, blade facing away from you, and tap down on the handle to get started.

- Repeat this process enough times to establish a split to a couple of inches (5cm) – or at least a split wide enough to insert your knife.

- Tuck your workpiece under your arm and hold it in your weaker hand.

- Insert the knife into the split and, using your other hand and twisting your wrist, begin to split. If the split begins to run off, push away the fattest side. (This looks a lot more dangerous than it really is, the knife is used only to split, not to slice. In fact, the blade can be reversed, so that the back of the knife faces the hand holding the rod.)

No amount of excellent splitting can cope with grain that is twisted or spiralled. When splitting well, the best you can hope to do is have the pith showing on both halves of your finished wood. This demonstrates that you've got the split as central as possible, so don't feel bad if you split something and it finishes off corkscrewed – it may not be your fault.

It is sometimes possible, if the material is particularly small or weak, to split and then correct a run-off using only your hands. This especially applies to splitting down roots, which are easy to control in the hand. It is also possible to do this by pushing the open split across a splitting post. This consists of a small stake, driven into the ground, with a triangular wedge created at the top of the stake point, facing towards the splitter. The opened rod is pushed against this triangle, and the craftsman leans to the right and left to keep the split central or correct any run-offs. This technique is ideal if you have many rods to cleave. In this scenario, setting up the stake is usually

1. Begin at the end, with your blade away from you.

2. Reverse the blade for safety and twist it, rather than pulling.

3. Lean on the fatter side of the split to prevent it running off. If you split a stick accurately in half, the pith will be visible.

4. Using a post to split rods.

5. The split stick.

much quicker than cleaving lots of rods in the hand – for some projects, the advantage of splitting may be as many as twice as many rods.

Certain shelter designs, particularly wigwams and benders, can be made from rods prepared in this way. Split wood also resists decay much longer than wood in the round.

Working With Large Timber

Once you move into the realms of larger timber, it is almost impossible to control the split if it runs off. You simply can't put enough force on the wood to even things up. In traditional green woodwork, craftsmen employed a tool called a 'froe', which can provide enough leverage to move quite substantial pieces of wood. However, the remit of this book is to cover techniques that can be used with a minimum of equipment.

Large-diameter wood of the type that you might choose for making a bow or a paddle, for example, is best split with axes, wedges or a combination of both. I have used two axes in the illustration below.

- Start by positioning the end of the log that is to be split against a backstop. This will prevent it moving as you try to force wedges into the end grain.

- Consider using an axe to score the entire length of the timber, by batoning the axe into the wood to a depth of half an inch (1.5cm) or so. (Although this is not always necessary, especially on very straight-grained timber, it does create a weakness that the split will tend to gravitate towards, rather than running off.)

- Drive an axe or a wedge into the top of the end grain, making sure you are dividing the wood completely in half.

- Work this split down, so that it covers the entire diameter of the wood. Only when the split is fully open should you place a wedge or axe directly into the end grain and try to advance the split down the timber. (If you start to split without ensuring that the end grain is open, you may find that the timber starts to quarter itself.)

1. Open the timber from the top edge.
2. Be sure that the end grain is open before continuing.
3. Leapfrog the tools down the stick.
4. Two equal halves should be produced.
5. Using a wooden wedge.

- Once the log is open, using a wedge, axe or combination of both, chase the split down the entire length of the workpiece. It is important not to jump too far ahead with the spacing of these two tools, as you might lose control of the split. If you do, your only option is to take your axe and baton it into the timber ahead of the problem, effectively creating a weakness that hopefully the split will gravitate towards. It is not always possible to do this: sometimes you have to accept that there will be some wastage – or smaller craft projects/firewood, as I like to call them.

Working With Smaller Timber

Smaller trees and branches can be felled effectively by batoning your knife through the stem. You may have to go several times around the circumference of the branch before it breaks. Personally, I'm not keen on this approach: I feel that harvesting should be done with a saw whenever possible, since this makes it much easier to make the correct pruning cuts and generally do a tidy job.

With small-diameter timber, it is possible to crosscut standing up, by holding the workpiece in your weaker hand, secured against your leg. Strike at an angle with your axe or billhook – important, as I've already mentioned, for severing all those spaghetti-like bundles of wood fibres – but make sure the tool will clear your legs once the wood has been cut. Again, you might have to rotate the timber, striking it from different angles around the circumference, to cut it completely through.

As mentioned previously, with some stubborn pieces of wood it may be prudent to go around its circumference twice or even three times. This is a heavy-duty version of the rose cut described earlier in the chapter.

As long as your legs are clear, it is possible to crosscut small-diameter wood while standing up.

Carving

Wood carving is immensely pleasurable. It is one of those activities that is quite easy to lose yourself in so completely that you suddenly realise several hours have passed. It reveals a world of patterns and interest, as the layers of the tree are stripped away in shaping your final piece. Insect damage, growth from good and bad years, branch scars, all might be found. Partially rotten wood also reveals the tree's efforts to seal out threats or where fungi has activated, split, formed alliances and finally left that characteristic spalting also known, rather evocatively, as 'fairy writing'. Sometimes these features are an annoyance, at other times they can be incorporated into the design of your work.

There are a couple of ways to approach any woodworking project. You can start a piece with a clear and fixed idea of exactly what you want to make, perhaps using scale drawings and exact dimensions. This is a great approach if uniformity is your goal; but a piece can be started with just a loose idea of what you want to make in your mind and then adapted to the variables found in the blank. I prefer the latter approach – it is a lot less frustrating!

Choosing Your Wood

Luckily, most smaller wood-carving projects require very little in terms of materials. It is certainly not necessary to take as much care as should be taken when making bows, for example. Often bendy, feature-filled blanks are the very thing needed to make a characterful and idiosyncratic item, yet this is the sort of material that would be another person's firewood.

For first attempts, as with bows, it is better to avoid pieces with too many features, especially in areas where the wood will narrow, such as the neck of a spoon. Species of tree vary in the degree of difficulty that you'll experience when carving them: some of the more robust wood for general utensils is tough as old boots and takes a good deal of effort to cut with hand tools. Such materials also take the edge off tools in double-quick time. So, in the early days of carving, compromise with less-dense wood, which undoubtedly is easier to carve. These include sycamore, willow and birch, all of which are ideal for the following projects.

Working with green wood is always easier than working with seasoned wood. The sap acts as a lubricant, helping the knife or axe to glide through the wood. As I repeat throughout this book, one of the principles of green woodworking is that movement, cracking and general warping occurs as the tree or piece of wood dries. This is because the outside of the tree is closer to the rest of the world, and therefore dries faster. This causes the outside surface to move, sometimes creating drying cracks, sometimes deforming the piece.

However, if a workpiece has been reduced to its almost-finished dimensions, there is very little difference between the inside and outside of the blank. Ninety-nine times out of 100, this should mean that the timber will dry without any problems. If you have to stop for any reason part-way through a project, consider slowing down the drying process by leaving your work in a moist environment. Traditionally, small items were placed in a bag with vegetable peelings to increase the ambient humidity.

Making Feather Sticks

This is a very useful little item to master, from a fire-making point of view, as well as a great way to learn knife control. If you don't have fine kindling, with a little skill and practice, eminently burnable alternatives can be made in the form of feather sticks. Fundamentally, a feather stick gives you both tinder in the form of its curls and kindling in the form of the stick from which it is made. Thus, the stick should be small enough to be ignited from the curls.

- To start, break a round of deadwood (see Chapter 1 on harvesting wood and Chapter 2 on using tools) into quarters, eighths or sixteenths, depending on the size you start with. You need to end up with pieces of wood with a triangular cross-section of around ¾in (19mm) across.

- Shave one of the triangular edges to make a flat platform, leaving two ridges on either side of this platform. If the weather has been bad, it is worth starting on the edge that was closest to the dry centre of the tree. By undercutting these ridges, very thin, easily burnt curls are produced – they can be thin because they are reinforced by a central spine created by the undercut ride.

- Keep rotating the workpiece, undercutting the edges and creating more, until the stick is about to break.

As always, the first key point when making a feather stick is choice of material. If your wood is too green, it will not curl; if it's seasoned to the point of decay, it will crumble. It is also difficult to create curls if you take too thick a slice or start too low down. Conversely, starting too high up makes a very long curl that is hard to control: I find around 6–8in (15 20cm) is enough. Keep the sticks long (12in or 30cm) for safety while carving, and so that you can move them easily once they're in a fire.

(From left to right) Split out a blank; create a platform; experiment with tilting the knife to pack in the curls; continue til the stick is about to break.

Ensure all curls are packed tight. In this example, the feather would burn without igniting the stick.

The aim is to produce a mass of tightly curled wood, all on the same side of the stick, with the final curl finishing within an inch or so (25mm) of the first. This gives a mass of heat, all in one place. Half a dozen of these sticks, together with small splints split off in the same way as the feather stick wood, should get the fire going. The small splints serve instead of secondary fuel. (See Chapter 6, in which all of this is covered when I discuss making fires.)

In addition, you may want to experiment with slotting curls into the end of your feather stick by varying the angle of your knife. Pointing the knife blade down sends curls to the right, while pointing the blade up sends them left and a level blade leaves them straight.

Making Spoons

It would appear from social media that this wonderful little pastime has turned into something of a wood-carving phenomenon: there are weekend courses, spoon meets, even shops specialising in hand-carved spoons. The great thing about spoons is that they are relatively quick to make to a high standard, and there is always the option of adding embellishments, should the carver wish to become a spoon-making ninja.

Fruit woods, such as cherry, apple and pear, are great for making spoons and other eating utensils, as the timber seems resistant to the wash-boarding effect caused by repeatedly getting the wood wet and dry through use. Unfortunately, they are also a little tough to carve, but this does allow them to be forced into interesting shapes, since the grain can be violated to some extent without risk of breakage.

With weaker woods, such as the ones mentioned already, it is better to look for twists and bends in the blanks rather than trying to force bends into the work. Imagine the wood fibres in a spoon blank running parallel from end to end. If a blank has a bend or kink in it, those wood fibres follow the kink, then so can the spoon. However, if the blank is straight and a bend is forced into it, the wood fibres may run out at this point, causing a weakness.

Many steps of the spoon-carving process were covered earlier in the knife-use section, but the following takes you through the techniques in depth and step-by-step:

- Start with a blank that has a reasonably clear feature that will add to the shape of the bowl. I look specifically for a small bend or kink, the start of which will form the neck of the spoon.

- The next step is to remove the pith – a dark line of spongy material in the centre of the blank, which is what remains of the tree before it became woody. (I like to get rid of this right away, especially from the bowl, and also to flatten out this area. That way, I can see exactly what I am left with.)

A nice blank.

- If the pith makes it all the way to the end of your workpiece, it might keep breaking out, leaving you with a two-pronged fork. Incidentally, with a large blank it is possible to keep splitting the halves to create a nest of spoons. Even without this, hopefully, you will have at least two options, although the top one will have the curve from the outside of the tree and will need flattening before you start work.

One of the secrets of carving spoons is working in only one dimension at a time, at least in the early stages. Another is not to be afraid of drawing your spoon's outline on the wood. At this point, you may wish to try the spoon nest technique, merely to make the whole blank thinner and easier to carve. Saw cuts and batoning, as well as chiselling, work well here, as do the reinforced and strangling techniques mentioned earlier, especially where the neck narrows.

- Leave the radius of the bowl until last, as it is easier to balance the spoon if it retains a square base. When you do come to this area, try laying your spoon flat and batoning it at an angle: it makes the bowl thinner, and therefore easier to carve the radius.

- Carve the radius by bracing the spoon with the thumb and carving gently towards yourself. This technique is not unlike peeling fruit, but for safety do have a dry run to ensure that you are clearing your hand with the knife, protecting yourself with the positioning of the spoon itself.

- Work the spoon as close to the lines as possible, then change to the other plane – drawing the shape once again will probably help. As you get closer to the finished item, all dimensions can be worked at the same time.

- Carve the bowl last, using a spoon gauge or crook knife. (I tend to use a crook knife in a potato-peeling mode, because I have found it neater to work the bowl from side to side, rather than up and down, when it tends to gouge.) Keep holding your spoon up to the light, and make sure that you stop well before you can see through it!

- Now sandpaper and a household, vegetable-based oil are all that are required (vegetable oils are non-toxic, which is important for eating utensils). You may or may not want to sand the whole thing – sometimes tool marks can be quite attractive – but I would advise you, for reasons of hygiene, to sand the inside of the bowl if you intend to eat with it.

1. Don't be afraid to mark out the work. Work in one plane only.

2–3. A spoon roughed out and marked out in the other plane.

4–5. Once the bulk of wood has been removed, you can start to work the spoon all over.

6. Using a crook knife.

7.From roughout to spoon.

Making Bowls and Cups

Counter-intuitively, bowls and cups should be carved into the split surface of a piece of wood, not the nice round end grain of the log. This is down to the way that wood moves as it dries (as previously discussed). Most of the movement when wood dries is tangential, so using the round part of a log generally results in severe cracking, leaky cups, wet legs and disappointment.

Not unlike spoons, cups can be as complicated as a person wants to make them; from simple, small dishes to a Scottish-style quaich with its elaborately carved handles.

If you can find them, a type of wood that is rather nice – especially for circular bowls – are the burrs that are often found on the sides of trees. These are areas of rapid and erratic cell division, usually caused by insects, fungi or bacteria. The wood in such areas can be spectacular, with intricate and swirling grain patterns.

! However, removing these burrs from a living tree will damage it severely, so only take them from trees that have been felled.

Unlike spoons, I usually make the bowl of a bowl first, as I find it much easier to hold the work steady if it's in a reasonably chunky state. Removing wood from the bowl can be done in the same way as described for spoons, but if you are feeling a little tired after all those spoons, you can also drill and chisel (or just chisel) out lots of wood in a relatively short time.

Once again, it is wise to work only one profile at a time. I start with the top view, then bring in the sides.

- If possible, split out a reasonably large piece, as it will be easier to control – this is especially true if you are using a gouge to make the bowl and an axe to remove the bulk of the wood. (Personally, I tend to saw off the blank when I am ready to move on to working with my knife.)

- With bowls – and to a lesser extent spoons – it may be worth producing an almost finished blank, then letting it dry a little before final finishing.

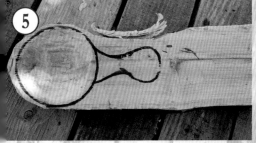

1. Don't be afraid to mark out the shape first.

2. Sometimes a spoon gouge is easier for large bowls.

3. Leaving a long stem can make tool work easier.

4. Stop cuts can also be made using an axe.

5. Attacking from both directions is the best way to work the curves. This is also true when using a knife to carve spoons.

(process continued overleaf)

- The right moment can be gauged by the amount of fluffing of the wood fibres that occurs when you try to satisfy the obsessive desire for a pristine surface (although perhaps that's just me!).

- Finish the bowl with a household vegetable oil (as mentioned previously, it is non-toxic). Some vegetable oils produce attractive stains and bring out the pattern in the wood, so do experiment.

Making Pot Hangers

Making implements on which to hang a brew pot is a must when you're out in the woods. They generally utilise a part of the fire that no one else wants, the bit directly above the flames, and can be set up so that the bulk of the hanger is downwind in the smoke, where no one wants to sit. For most of these projects, hazel is my wood of choice. It is freely available in most areas and produces interesting straights, hooks and convenient branching structures, all in a range of very useful diameters.

My favourite such implement is the ingenious whagon stick, with its elegant design and cunning hanging device. Use wood of a diameter that matches the size of the pot you are using. Bushcraft should be elegant and hanging a 1-litre (0.2 gallon) pot on a 2in (5cm) diameter hanger just looks wrong. Set yourself the challenge, too, of getting all the component parts from one stem. Whagon sticks can be made very delicate, in which case it will probably take you around three months of use before the device is trusted not to drop your meal in the fire.

6. It is possible to get close to the lines with an axe.

7. Work the side profile after you've worked the front.

8. Cut off the stem when it's time to use your knife.

9. Once you've made a blank, consider letting it dry.

10. Ready for finishing.

11. Oiled and sanded.

The Beak Cut
Most of the skills needed for this little project have been explained already, with the exception of the beak cut.

- For this, make an X-cut into your workpiece, then cut each side of the 'X' to create a V-cut.

- Carry on removing wood by cutting the 'V' and shaving up to it. Little and often is the secret here, don't be tempted to use lots of force. This process can be continued until the cut almost reaches the halfway point.

- There will be a ridge in the middle of the cut, which can now be removed by undercutting it and the beak that has been formed. It is important to undercut this beak to create a point: this will help balance the hanger.

The beak thus created fits into the end of the crane, which should be shaped like a screwdriver head and have a small indent carved into it to accept the beak. When making the screwdriver head, offset the angle at which the end is sharpened. This is to avoid making the indent into the pith, which may break out and spill your meal.

The hook on the bottom of the hanger can be made either from a convenient twig or an X-cut, carved facing upwards. It is important that the hook and the hanging notches are both on the same side of the stick, for added stability. Several beaks can be carved for adjustable cooking heights.

The horizontal element of the hanger should be as straight as possible – which, in fact, is virtually impossible to find. Bearing this in mind, place the horizontal across the upright to establish where it naturally wants to sit – this is to avoid the horizontal twisting once it is in use.

The upright is a forked stick, sharpened into a stake that can be driven into the ground and with a top that is bevelled to resist shattering. Ideally, the fork will be made from a horizontal branch as opposed to a true fork, as this means that when it is driven into the ground, the place where it is being hit is more in line with the base of the stake: open forks often split when they are being driven into the ground. The base of the horizontal can be held down using two sticks, a dead man's finger, or just weighted down with a log.

aking the beak cut.

1. Offset the end to avoid the pith.
2. Make a shallow indent to accept the hanger.
3. The hanger beak fits snugly on the horizontal.
4. Select a stake with a side branch to avoid breaking the fork.
5. Twin pegs or a single dead man's finger can be used to pin down the horizontal.
6. A finished whagon stick.

The Crane
An alternative to this set-up is the crane, which requires a good eye for various shapes and the knowledge of how to make a withy or use a root – useful skills in their own right (they are described in detail in Chapter 5). The beauty of a crane is that it can be scaled up to hold some really quite substantial pots and will make a long-lasting item that can be used again and again.

Very robust versions can be made with group cooking in mind. A simple carved indent at the top of the stake, to aid tying the crane to the upright, and an X-cut at the end of the crane to accept the pot are pretty much all that is needed, assuming of course, that you have managed to find a suitably shaped piece of wood.

Your wood needs to fork into two branches, one of which must fork again, but this time at 90° to the original branch; fortunately, hazel lends itself to this branching habit. A further X-cut on the non-forked branch of the crane allows you to tie these two elements together, using a root, withy or any other spare cord you happen to have hanging around, including any bits of bark left over from your craft efforts.

The second fork then sits against the upright, allowing the whole thing to swivel. The downside of this arrangement is that there is no scope for height adjustment, but you can move a pot in and out of the flames, although a small stick may be necessary to hold the crane in position, as it may swing back into the flames when you don't want it to. (Incidentally, I have used a similar arrangement to this in a tepee but providing a single central pole on which to hang lanterns.)

!   The key to all these methods is to use green wood and leave the bark on – this gives the devices longevity by the fire.

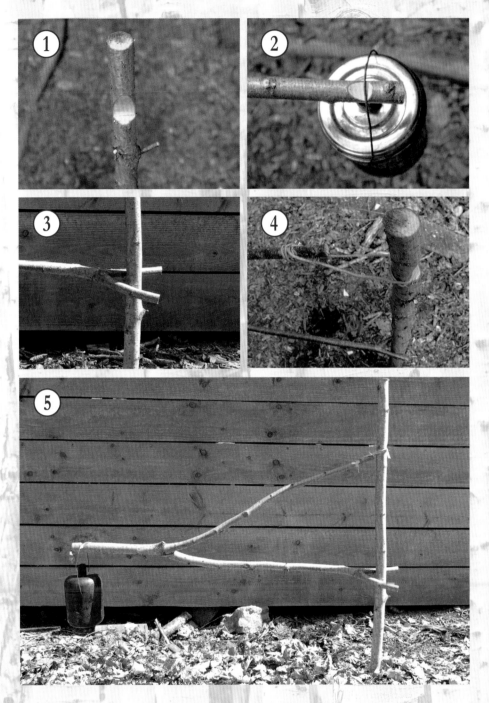

1. Drive the stake into the ground and cut a notch to hold the binding.

2. Cut a notch to accept the pot.

3. The lower fork swivels against the upright.

4. Tie the two elements together. In this case, I am using a root.

5. A finished crane.

4

Bow-Making

Like many people, I first made bows as a child, using bits of kite string tied to willow or hazel wands, with those green garden canes for arrows. These, mixed with shop-bought kits consisting of a plastic bow and several arrows fitted with rubber suction cups, were soon combined into a schoolboy arsenal.

As I grew older and stronger, I became increasingly dissatisfied with the 30ft (10m) range and lack of power. Discovering that it was quite easy to remove the rubber caps from the arrows, and that it took only minutes to sharpen the wooden shafts by rubbing them on the pavement, I increased the penetrative power of the weapons tenfold.

This was great until I tested their power on the backside of my older sister. At point-blank range, to my considerable surprise, the arrow stuck and held in her flesh, albeit briefly. Unfortunately – but somewhat predictably – this led to parents getting involved and my arsenal was duly confiscated. However, I guess the spark of inspiration remained, and many years later I started to make grown-up bows, partly as a study of trees and timber, and partly for the romance and historic thrill of this weapon of the woodsman.

Shooting a bow.

A Note on Measurement

Many traditional crafts have their roots way back in history, and certainly before the metric system became common in the UK. I have converted the measurements roughly from imperial to metric for marking out the bows, and when describing length of arrows and fletching. The draw weights of bows are still measured in pounds (lb) and certainly if one tried to buy a weapon in kilograms, your average bowyer would not really know what you meant. This is also true when describing the diameter of commonly used arrow shafts and the spine weights, as they match the draw weights of the bows.

Types of Bows

There are many different types of bows from all over the world, but I have always been fascinated with all-wood, straight-stave bows: that is, bows that have no special adornments, curves, reflexes or add-ons. I have experimented with other types over the years. I have used steam-bending techniques to shape bows to resemble the classic weapons of Mongolia and Turkey. I have used sinew and rawhide to mimic bows from tree-poor regions.

However, because I live and work in northern Europe, I have access to a documented heritage and rich tradition of all-wood bows. This tradition favours such weapons because we are rich in wood, in terms of both quantity and quality. Bows of mixed materials, usually called composite bows, tend to originate in areas of poor-quality timber where reinforcement is required to prevent breakages. Either that, or the lengths that are available are so short they must be coupled with more elastic materials to make them strong enough to be drawn back to a decent arrow length without giving way.

Straight-stave bows form two basic types: longbows and flatbows. Surprisingly, what makes a longbow a longbow isn't necessarily its length. After all, every wooden bow must reach a sufficient length to be able to take significant strain on its limbs without causing it to break. If your bow is only 5ft (1.5m) long, pulling far enough back to shoot a 32in (81cm) arrow probably is going to be a big ask.

What really makes a longbow a longbow is that its cross-section is almost as deep as it is wide. In fact, the British Longbow Society states that a longbow's thickness should be at least five-eighths of its width. Traditionally, the cross-section of a longbow is D-shaped. This would have the flat part of the 'D' as the back of the bow (the bit closest to the target), and the rounded part of the 'D' as the belly (the bit closest to the archer).

There are two distinct types of longbows that are most often discussed: the recreational target bow and the artillery-style war bow of the Hundred Years' War. However, there are also examples of narrow-limbed, D-cross-sectioned bows dating back into the distant archaeological record, suggesting that this style of bow has been with us since the earliest development of such weapons. Although its journey to the bows of the present day is neither direct nor easy to follow, it would appear that the heavy longbow famous from Crécy and Agincourt had its roots in the Stone Age, in reality changing only slightly in response to fresh military advances.

The history of the longbow isn't my area of expertise. If you're particularly interested, many eminent writers have already covered the subject (see the Further Reading section at the end of this book), but the brief version is that as armour became more advanced, bows became more powerful, so that longer and heavier arrows could be shot safely. The longer the arrow, the further you could draw the bow, thus the more energy would be stored by the bow. All things being equal, this would impart more energy to the arrow on release, leading to greater effective range and penetration. To draw these bows further back, they were made longer, so the physical effort involved in drawing them back (their draw weight) was increased, again leading to more energy storage. With these two factors at play, increasingly chunky and robust weapons were developed.

The second type of wooden bow in this chapter is the flatbow, so-called because it is wider than it is deep. Within this group are many variations, ranging from the sophisticated Mollegabet and Holmegaard bows through to simple, very wide, paddle-shaped Meare Heath versions.

Many different bow designs are found across the northern hemisphere.

Unfortunately, few timbers are strong or dense enough to be made into narrow cross-section longbows. Flatbows spread the compression and tension forces across a wider area, meaning that a wider array of wood is available to the bow maker. This spreading of forces also means that, in general, flatbows can be made shorter relative to their draw weight and length of arrow (draw length).

I have made lots of longbows and flatbows, in several designs. I love the simplicity of the longbow's design and its history, which ranges from the 6,000 year old Rotten Bottom bow, a weapon from the Mesolithic period, through to the hunting weapon of the woodsman, and then beefed-up military bows. However, I also love the various flatbow designs and the hunter-gatherer feel of these weapons, together with the arguably better accuracy when shooting. I will explore both over the following pages.

Choosing Your Timber

To begin, we need to get a couple of things straight, especially if you are new to bow-making. It is unlikely that the new archer will want to shoot – or indeed enjoy shooting – a 170lb (77kg) monster of a bow that is capable of pinning a charging knight to his horse. In fact, the upper end of the estimated draw weight for medieval war bows is a matter of some controversy among bow-makers and historians alike. It seems unlikely that the actual weapons were of the colossal poundage that many have described. (Forgive me, but I don't intend to open that particular can of worms here: there are many authorities you can go to who discuss the pros and cons of these claims in detail – see the Further Reading section.)

Similarly, be aware that unless it is the medieval style of shooting that you are interested in, or you drag your knuckles along the floor as you walk – you are unlikely to have a massive draw length. There is a particular style of drawing: for example, an artillery bow to a 32in (81cm) or longer arrow, which demands drawing the arrow so far back that it is termed 'shooting in the bow', as the archer is positioned somewhat in-between the bow and the extended string.

In normal shooting, shorter arrows are used and drawn to a consistent point on the head or face, but with the archer topside of the string. Most people will start with a relatively low-weight bow, probably no heavier than 50lb (23kg) – in some cases, significantly less. I have a friend who decided he was going to shoot very heavy longbows, and eventually he did end up pulling weapons of 150lb (68kg) plus. Be warned: it took him nine different bows, of gradually increased weights, to get to that weight. If this is something that you wish to pursue, I'll just say, please take your time. In the best-case scenario, you are likely to develop poor shooting technique due to being overloaded; in the worst-case scenario, you could cause yourself significant injury.

Wood Density and Elasticity

There are several options when it comes to choosing suitable timber for the construction of a bow. In essence, considering the narrow cross-section of a longbow, we need woods that are relatively high density. This means that the woods have more fibres in a given area than low-density timber. This is the difference between a wood such as willow (low density) and oak (high density).

However, identifying a species as high-density is only the start, as variation exists between individual trees. It is possible to judge density to some extent by the growth of annual rings: with conifers, such as the bowyer's favourite yew, the rule of thumb is the tighter the annual rings, the denser the timber. Confusingly, with broad-leafed trees, the opposite is true.

It is actually a little more complicated than this, but for now (and to avoid going into the major distinctions), this is a decent starting point. Anyone who is interested in taking this subject further will need a study of diffuse, ring-porous, semi-ring-porous and non-porous wood; work on ratios of spring and summer wood also would be worthwhile (see the Further Reading section).

It is possible, if low-density woods are all that you can find, to make bows that are longer and/or wider, effectively taking the strain off this weaker wood. However, there is a point where this becomes counterproductive and may force a design change. The longbow's narrow-section design may not be the best for very weak woods, which would be better suited to flatbows. It could be that, even then, the bow has to be so wide or long as to be ungainly or even ugly – I feel it is important to make any piece of craftwork as elegant as possible.

Wood density isn't the only criterion: we must also consider the elasticity of the wood. Some very dense woods really don't like being bent, and we are aiming *not* to finish up, at the far end of the bow-making process, with two separate pieces of wood or some very elaborately carved firewood!

Species I have used with success include:

- American red oak
- ash
- hawthorn
- hazel
- holly
- laburnum
- rowan
- field maple
- walnut
- wych elm
- yew.

Of course, if you can find it, yew is widely considered the ultimate material. Indeed, it was the timber of choice for medieval bowyers and is found far back in the archaeological record, with yew weapons having been discovered that were made in the Mesolithic period.

My tree list is by no means exhaustive, so there are plenty of other woods with which you may wish to experiment. I've had some small success with cherry and feel that the wood of some other fruit trees, such as apple and pear, would be worth trying. However, I would especially like to try to make a bow from blackthorn, should I ever manage to find the long, straight and clean length I need for the purpose.

Sizing It Up

To make a longbow, you will need to find timber at least 6½ft (1.98m) in length, preferably slightly longer. Timber perhaps 7½ft (2.28m) long will allow for drying cracks at the ends of the stave, which, on cleft timber, rarely penetrate more than a few inches and can be removed when you cut the bow to its final length after drying.

The finished length of a longbow should really be a minimum of 6ft (1.82m). These measurements can be scaled down for a flatbow, although I would suggest for a first bow, a minimum finished length of no less than 68in (1.72m) and would try to season a stave 6ft (1.82m) long at the very least.

A few ash staves, ready to go.

For the time being, perhaps the most widely available bow-quality timber in the UK is ash. However, this may change as we wait to see the extent of ash dieback – a disease that seems to be sweeping the country.

When making bows, it makes sense to try to make the back of the bow as flat as possible. This is the face furthest away from the archer, while the belly is the bit closest. In practice, this means finding a tree with a relatively large diameter, since this gives a shallow curve on the circumference of the tree, and this gentle curve will lead to a flatter cross-section. Bear in mind that for the weapons I am describing, the back of the bow is made from the surface of the tree directly under the bark. This means that it should have a completely intact annual ring, which – when put under tension as the bow bends – is less likely to snap than a stave that has had this pristine surface hacked at, potentially allowing the fibres to lift.

The rationale behind using the outer part of the tree as the back of the bow takes into consideration how trees move in the wind. If you imagine a tree rocking backwards and forwards, the part closest to the centre of the tree compresses, while the outer layer stretches. This is exactly how we want our bow to behave. In some trees, there is a distinct difference between this outer area, often wrongly called sapwood (it carries water and nutrients, not sap) and the heartwood. Regardless of whether this distinction can be spotted (it is obvious with yew, for example), fibres will still be orientated to this motion.

Although larger-diameter trees give you the best chance of making a successful bow on your first attempt, do remember that it is possible to make perfectly functional longbows from smaller-diameter timber. Just be aware that the more steeply curving outside of the tree, which forms the back of your bow, detracts from the very rectangular cross-section we know to be strongest.

Ideally, look for a fairly large-diameter ash tree, or something similar. Once felled, it must be split into quarters, possibly eighths, depending on its original diameter. We want to finish up with a blank that is perhaps 1½in (38mm) to 1 in (44mm) across the back of the bow for a longbow, maybe 2in (5cm) for a flatbow.

The blank should have relatively straight sides, 90° to the back of the bow – this is important. While cleaving wood, it is very easy to create a wedge and, if your blank tapers to any degree, you could end up with the sides of your bow sloping so abruptly into the belly that you cannot produce the required profile.

For your first longbow, the longer the blank, the better: 6ft (1.82m) should be considered the minimum. Some efficiency would be lost with a longer bow, but nonetheless go for 6ft 6in (1.98m) if you have enough timber. This will allow the bow to be under less strain when bent, as there will be more working limb to take the load.

There is a slight trade-off here: the extra wood creates mass that the bow has to move forward using energy that otherwise would be available to the arrow. The reality is that unless you are already an experienced archer, you are unlikely to notice this reduction in speed and efficiency. (If you're anything like I was when I was making my first bow, you might just be delighted to get to the stage of shooting an arrow at all!)

This trade-off has been something of an issue for longbow-makers throughout history. As we have already discussed, making the arrow longer and drawing the bow back further to accommodate this arrow length always meant that the bow had to be longer to take the strain. However, the increased mass of the limbs becomes counterproductive once you get towards 7ft (2.13m) in length, as the increased draw weight doesn't mean that arrows fly all that much further, due to the energy-robbing increase in mass.

Seasoning the Timber

The first thing to do to with the blank is remove the bark, partly because this is so much easier when the bark is fresh. It also allows the bow to dry more quickly and evenly. With this in mind, I try to fell bow staves in early spring, while the moisture in the wood is sufficient to loosen the bark, but the birds haven't started nesting yet, so I don't risk disturbing them with felling operations. Be very careful not to dig into the wood itself while removing the bark: it creates a place where fibres could potentially lift.

It's worth thinking about seasoning the timber at this point, but it isn't necessary to leave bow staves out for several years before they can be worked. Instead, it is quite possible on the day that you fell a stave to rough out to almost finished proportions. Just allow it to dry before the final finishing-off process.

As mentioned in Chapter 3, this is possible because of the way that wood moves while it is drying. Most of this movement is tangential, which is what you see as splits and drying cracks if you look down on the end of a log. The outside of the tree is closer to the rest of the world than the inside and therefore dies faster, causing movement. This not only produces drying cracks in logs, but also may cause twisting and warping. One of the principles of working wood while it is green or fresh and unseasoned is the production of a blank or rough-out that, by having removed as much wood as possible, lessens the difference between the inside and outside of that piece. This should mean that there is less chance of cracking and twisting because the wood will dry much more evenly.

Once you have got your bow down to almost finished dimensions, you must stop and wait for it to dry completely before bending it. This is vital: if wood for a bow is bent when it's still green, it will stay bent even when the bowstring is removed (see the description below on string follow).

Using this method, it is possible to go from felled trees to finished bow in as little as a couple of weeks. It depends very much on the ambient temperature and humidity of your environment. I do not recommend force drying, even when trying to make a bow quickly, and I am quite careful where I dry the wood. Avoid sheds and free-standing garages, for example, as they heat up and cool down to extremes. If you have a cool spare room or a garage that is attached to the house, so that the fluctuations in temperature are less pronounced, these are ideal places to store your staves as they dry, putting them under the bed, resting on smaller logs to get the air flowing underneath

Laminated Wood and Working with Yew

Many people use laminated wood to make bows. This mimics what is happening naturally in the tree: gluing tough, tension-resistant wood onto dense, compression-resistant wood recreates the natural fibre-orientation of the inside and outside of a tree. Using laminated wood also allows you to make bows from otherwise unsuitable pieces of wood.

I have experimented with laminates a good deal in the past – indeed, my first bows were made from lemon wood and hickory – but now I rarely use them for ecological reasons. Many of the species used in this way come from abroad, which can leave a heavy carbon footprint. As well as being able to sustainably source my own timber, I find it much more pleasurable to work the woods in my own locale, creating that link back into the distant past. It is also incredibly satisfying to be able to take in the whole process, from harvesting the wood to finishing your bow.

Some of you may be lucky enough to come across some more favoured bow wood, such as yew. If you are a novice and you come across a cracking stave, I suggest you put it to one side and make several bows with other, less rare and more affordable species. Yew is very difficult to find in a suitable condition for bow-making, at least in the UK, and it would be a shame to waste it through inexperience.

Aside from its value and rarity, yew wood can be lumpy, bumpy and quite difficult to work. I still remember a piece that I was given way back in my early days of making longbows, which I completely ruined as I really didn't know what I was doing. Sometimes I still think about that piece of wood and imagine what I could have made with it later, once my knowledge and experience had increased. It is a regret that I am glad to be able to warn you against.

An unusually small amount of sapwood for a UK yew.

Should you manage to find a nice piece of yew, the other problem you will come across is the amount of sapwood compared to heartwood. Probably because of the wet and mild climate in the UK, yew tends to grow very quickly and produce an enormous amount of sapwood. Just to clarify these archaic terms: sapwood is the white or creamy-coloured wood on the outside of the tree, whose fibres are orientated in tension and are not good in compression.

If you imagine a longbow tapering from the handle on the belly-side towards the back, it is quite possible that towards the ends of the bow you can end up with all sapwood and no heartwood, should the former be very thick. With flatbow designs it can be even worse, with entire limbs made of sapwood. This can lead to string follow, compression frets (see below) or even breakages.

Sometimes it is better to remove some, if not all, of the sapwood, and have either an all-heartwood bow, or one where you have followed an annual ring faithfully all the way down the length of the stave, leaving the sapwood approximately ¼in (6mm) thick. This is quite hard work and, to be honest, not something for which I really have the patience. Heartwood-only bows work fine, and that would be my choice – but if you were in any doubt, you could always glue some backing wood onto the back of the stave.

String Follow, Deflex and Reflex

String Follow

Before going any further, I will explain string follow, as it does relate to timber selection. If your bow has set or string follow, even with the bowstring removed, the bow will still look bent towards the body of the archer. One of the things that makes a bow efficient is how hard the limbs are made to work. As the bow is drawn, the limbs come under strain and start to store energy. A bow that is completely straight won't be working quite so hard as a bow with limbs facing forward or reflexed. But would still be storing more energy than a bow with limbs bent back towards the archer, or deflexed, as with string follow.

Deflex

Deflex can be found naturally in wood, but the bow-maker should avoid putting it in artificially, either by bending the wood when it is still green or making some other mistake during the roughing out or tillering processes. If you do split out staves and they are deflexed, it is possible to clamp them when they're drying, and this will take out the excessive bend to some extent. In addition, you can heat the wood up and force a bend into it in the opposite direction, even to the point of making it reflexed. (Once again, I have tried all these approaches over the years, but have concluded it is much better just to find a decent piece of wood in the first place, rather than trying to adapt one that isn't quite right.)

Reflex

You could be forgiven for assuming that a stave with a natural reflex (bent away from the archer) would be the ultimate starting point, and in many ways, you are correct. You will have a much more efficient energy-storing spring that, in turn, makes more energy available to the arrow than any other naturally occurring feature. However, extremely reflex bows are much harder to make, especially for the novice, as you have to guess how much of the bow is reflex and how much of the bow is draw weight during the tillering process – the guess is often wrong. Deflexed bows are considered by many as easier bows to shoot accurately. Some bowyers will even build in a small amount of string follow to improve accuracy in this way.

* * *

In summary, I recommend that for a first bow you find a 6½ft (1.98m) stave for a longbow (less for a flatbow), from a fairly large-diameter tree that is either straight or perhaps only slightly reflexed in profile.

Roughing Out

Once the tree has been selected, felled, its bark removed and, finally, split into quarters, the amount of timber still left to be removed can seem quite daunting. Depending on how much wood remains, chipping away with a small axe can be quite efficient; however, perhaps a better approach is to make a series of saw cuts close to the finished dimensions, then chisel the wood out from between the cuts by batoning, either with a knife or an axe.

Caution must be taken when removing timber in this way. Do not try to take the wood exactly to the finished dimensions in one go: it might take two or even three attempts to remove the unwanted material. By taking your time, you will avoid – or at least make less likely – undercutting the saw cut and splitting chunks of bow out by mistake.

This series of reduction saw cuts can be carried out in each plane of the bow. Try to make, at least initially, a fairly rectangular piece of wood 1½in (38mm) to 1¾in (45mm) in diameter, and 6ft (1.82m) or more long, by 1in (25mm) to 1½in (38mm) deep. Of course, this also will have had its bark removed, and it should probably be left somewhat over the intended length to allow for drying cracks.

Before any of this can be achieved, it's important to check the stave thoroughly for excessive twists or bends. A slight propeller twist at the ends is quite common, especially with ash trees, and is normally not a problem, but in very severe cases this may result in the bow trying to turn itself inside out as it bends – which is difficult to correct but amusing for passers-by.

Look down the stave from top to toe and you should be able to see twists and dog legs caused by the orientation of the grain. These are much harder to deal with when it comes to making the bowstring line up with the centre of your finished bow. Although it isn't essential, your life will be made much easier if the bowstring passes fairly close to the centre point of the stave, at least through the handle section. However, it is worth noting

Reducing the timber using stop cuts.

that some people do make bows with the string pushed slightly to one side, with a view to making their bow either left or right-handed. This avoids the archer's paradox (which I will explore in more detail, when discussing arrows later in this chapter).

If you become interested in experimenting, there will be staves aplenty in the category of 'characterful'. I think it's a phase bow-makers need to go through, and I spent a good deal of time challenging myself to make bows from frankly unsuitable pieces of wood. Nowadays, I really can't be bothered. I always make life easier and go for the best stave I possibly can.

Once your stave has been roughed to the dimensions described above, you can start to lay out the bow. This is best achieved by first establishing a centre line. It is unlikely you will have a pristine piece of wood that looks like it has come straight from the hardware store, so taking dimensions from the centre line hopefully will give a more accurate measurement. Using a piece of string is still probably the most effective way of doing this.

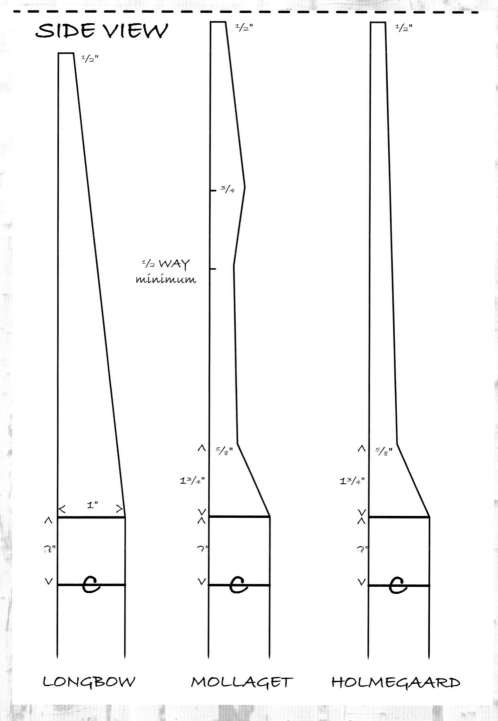

SIDE VIEW

½"

½ WAY
minimum

< 1" >
∧
3"
∨

LONGBOW

½"

3/4

∧ 5/8"
1 3/4"
∨
∧
3"
∨

MOLLAGET

½"

∧ 5/8"
1 3/4"
∨
∧
3"
∨

HOLMEGAARD

Bow dimensions.

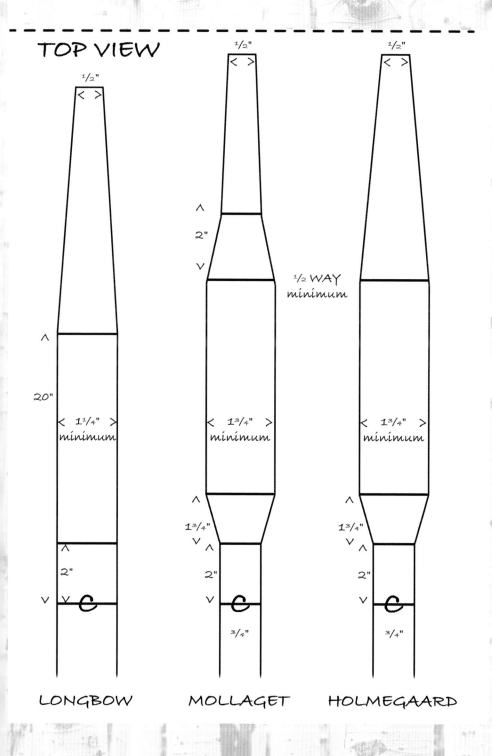

TOP VIEW

1/2"
< >

1/2"
< >

1/2"
< >

^
2"
v

1/2 WAY
minimum

^
20"
v

< 1 1/4" >
minimum

< 1 3/4" >
minimum

< 1 3/4" >
minimum

^
1 3/4"
v
^
2"
v

^
1 3/4"
v
^
2"
v

^
2"
v

3/4"

3/4"

LONGBOW

MOLLAGET

HOLMEGAARD

Once you have marked the centre line using the string and joined the dots, your next job is to find the exact midpoint of the limb, which will be somewhere around 3ft (0.9m) on a 6ft (1.82m) stave. At this point, things vary considerably, depending on whether you are making a longbow or a flatbow.

Longbows

With the centre line in place, it's time to decide how traditional your bow is to be, since medieval-style longbows don't have a handle in the centre. At the time, it was thought to be more important that the arrow passed as close to the halfway point of the bow as possible when it was shot. With this in mind, the 4in (10cm) handle section would run from 1in (25mm) above to 3in (7.5cm) below the true centre of the bow (or thereabouts).

There are pros and cons to this approach. It is possible – and arguably, desirable – to make a centre-shot weapon, by measuring 2in (5cm) either side of the dead centre of the bow for your handle. This approach certainly makes some things easier – especially tillering, where part of the process is ensuring that both limbs bend correctly and evenly.

With centre-shot bows, it can be simpler to make sure that the bottom and the top limb match as a smooth arc. With an offset, medieval-style handle, the lower limb bends slightly less and is under more strain, so will appear shorter and stiffer than the upper limb. In fact, you want to produce a slightly asymmetrical arc or tiller for a traditional longbow. Moreover, centre-shot bows can be turned upside down, which is handy because, being a natural material, wood sometimes shoots better one way around than another.

Nonetheless, I mostly make longbows in the traditional manner, and the one laid out in the illustrations has been made in this way.

Dimensions
Before getting too involved in laying out the dimensions of the bow, it is important to realise that there have never been set measurements that indicate a true English longbow. I have been lucky enough to see bows pulled out of the Solent with the wreck of the *Mary Rose*, Henry VIII's flagship. This boat contained many intact yew bows from the period, just before the longbow ceased to be used as a serious military weapon, and therefore

was probably at its zenith in terms of development. These discoveries most likely give an accurate historical snapshot of the military war bow of old.

While the variations in length of these weapons are worth noting, it is perhaps more interesting that there are also variations in cross-section. Many – in fact, the vast majority – do appear to be D-sectioned, just as longbows are today, but there are also round cross-sections and ones that are almost square, with just the corners rounded off. To me, this illustrates masters of the craft getting the best possible weapon from each piece of wood by adapting to a stave's individual character.

Often, the taper of these weapons is not evident right from the handle, with many bows showing little or no tapering on the back of the bow for a good proportion of their length, before narrowing down to the tips. This makes perfect sense, as the main working part of the limb is the bit from the handle to perhaps 8 or 10in (20–25cm) from the tip. This is the area that takes the most strain and stores most of the bow's energy, so keeping it as wide as possible, for as long as possible, demonstrates a thorough understanding of bow mechanics.

Indeed, non-working tips that are used as levers are a consideration for every all-wood bow design, including flatbows, as we will soon discover.

!   Remember, it is only possible to bend short pieces of wood so far before they break.

Again, the weight of the bow limbs and their potential to rob the arrow of energy in being moved forward themselves, especially when this dead weight is placed at the ends of the bow's limbs, is important. The limb tips travel furthest on release, so they require lots of energy to be moved. Therefore, limb tips should be made light, but rigid.

Following the example of the *Mary Rose*, my absolute preference for a longbow is for the central 40in (1m) to be the same width, regardless of whether the bow is centre-shot or offset at the handle. This arrangement gives maximum strength across the main working part of the limb, while retaining the opportunity to keep the limb tips nice and light. It is possible to taper the bow directly from the handle to the tip – many fine bows are made this way – but heavy bows, those under a great deal of strain, are perhaps better with wide working parts, even if this does mean a slight increase in overall mass.

Of course, with the sorts of draw weights we're talking about, it could well be argued that widening the centre section is overkill. However, with your first bow, your preference should be for a bow that has a reduced chance of breaking, rather than one that is pushed to its limit.

The width depends heavily on the tree species chosen for your wood. I find with ash that 1 1/8 to 1¼ in (28–32mm) at the handle section is more than enough. If you are building a giant-slaying bow of heroic proportions, then 1½in (37mm) would be ideal; with a good clean stave of ash around 6½ft long (1.98), this would be possible.

Whichever you choose, the next step is to mark out a 4in (10cm) handle section either 2in (5cm) above and 2in (5cm) below the centre point or, as discussed above, 1in (25mm) above and 3in (7.5cm) below.

Should you choose the traditional offset handle, there are things that may influence your decision as to which end of the stave should be the top and the bottom. Aside from general preference, you'll need to consider features within the wood: if you have knots, wild grain or anything else that's likely to weaken the bow, it makes sense to put them in the upper limb, as this is under slightly less strain than the shorter and stiffer lower limb.

Marking Out the Longbow

To mark out, follow this process:

- Measure 20in (50cm) either side of the centre-point of the bow. This entire portion of both limbs needs to be the width that you have selected at the handle, based on the final desired draw weight of the bow.

- At the very end of the bow, measure ½in (12mm) overall, in other words, ¼in (6mm) either side of the centre line.

- Draw a line from this point to the 20in (50cm) mark in a smooth taper. You may wish to allow a little bit more for any poor carpentry and make the ends of the limb initially at least 5/8 in (14–16mm) in overall thickness.

- Once you've done so, repeat on the other limb.

The top view of a marked-out longbow.

Should you choose to draw an even taper from the handle, this should start right at the end of your handle mark, regardless of whether you have an offset or a centred handle, and run up to the thickness mark at the limb tip

Working the Longbow

Before we start removing wood, a brief word is needed concerning knots. Live knots – those that aren't obviously black and old – are less of an issue than dead knots. Generally, small knots are not a huge problem, although it does depend on where they are within the limb. All knots are less of a problem when they're in the centre of the limb, rather than when they're on the edge.

Should you find a knot on the edge of your bow limb, you may have to build some wood around the knot to help support it. This may also dictate whether you taper a bow from the handle section or leave the working part the same linear width throughout. It obviously makes little sense to cut through the side of a knot, forcing it to the edge of the bow, just for the stake of creating a taper. This is easier to see than read about, as these images show.

Now, with the bow's dimensions established and drawn in, you can begin to remove everything that isn't a bow. How much material needs to be removed will determine your choice of tools: sawing or batoning, axing or draw knifing is up to you.

- Take the wood to the point where the marked-out lines just start to disappear. Of course, the closer you get to this line, the finer the tool you need to be using. Unless you've got incredible control, it is unlikely you'll be able to finish the entire bow using only an axe.

149

- You are aiming for a stave with the correct taper (looking on to the back of the bow) and with the sides tapering down perpendicular to the back.

- I encourage you to draw your marks on the back of the bow, as they serve as a reminder not to gouge or mess in any other way with the surface, which we are trying to keep pristine at all costs.

Once you have made this first taper, it is time to flip the bow over and draw the second taper, starting from the belly and moving to the tips. At this point, you can make another decision about how traditional you would like to be.

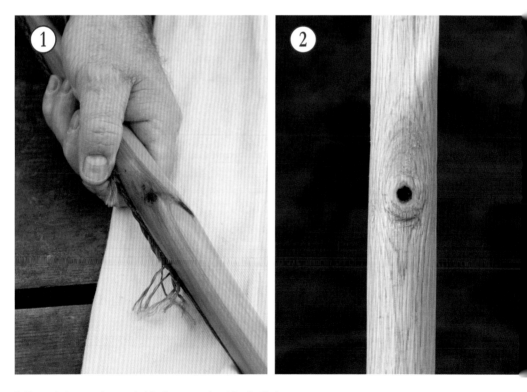

1. Extra timber may be needed for knots on the side of a limb.

2. Islands of wood can be left to support knots in the centre of the bow limb.

Traditional longbows bent right into the handle, which in practice meant that there was no real discernible lump in the centre section, so that the bow was free to work in this area. Later longbows and flatbows have a stiffened handle section: the rationale is that a stabilisation effect is produced by having a stiffened handle centre section. (I'm not entirely sure this is correct: it seems to make no difference, but then that could just be my bad shooting.) However, what I do understand is that the handle effectively gives you less working limb, and thus more strain is placed on the limbs. (This may be another reason why war bows bent through the handle: adding this feature to the extra width and length we have already discussed, medieval bowyers were most likely making sure that they put the maximum amount of wood to work, storing energy and spreading the forces.)

In this design, we will be following the medievalists:

- Mark your 4in (10cm) handle section on the side of the bow stave (regardless of whether it's offset or centre-shot).

- Draw these lines from the back of the bow to the belly, on both sides. At the end of the 4in (10cm) section, mark 1in (25mm). Do this for both ends of the handle.

- At the very tips of the bow, mark down another ½in (12mm). (Once again, if you're nervous about your carpentry skills, initially mark 5/8 in (14–16mm).

- Join the lines from the end of the handles to the tips of the bow.

- If you want your bow to bend through the handle in the traditional style – as we're doing in this description – carry the depth from one end of the handle to the other, thus creating a central 4in (10cm) x 1in (25mm) handle section. If you want the handle to be stiffened in the centre section, then leave this 4in (10cm) section as thick as is comfortable to hold.

Establishing this taper can be quite difficult. As the 'back' of your bow is unlikely to be smooth and straight, like a freshly planed piece of 2 x 2, trying to put together an accurate taper line can be very difficult. It's also quite likely that you will have some reflex or defects, even if very slight. Laying a straight edge from the tip to the handle will probably result in an uneven taper: thick in some places and thin in others. Obviously, this is not ideal for a longbow, as it will be stiffer in the thick spots and bend too much in the thin.

One solution is to draw the length and depth of your bow out on a piece of wood that you know is straight. Then, transfer the measurements from that piece of wood onto your bow stave, measuring accurately every 4 to 6in (10–15cm), and joining short lines together to create the taper.

The other option is to do it by eye: use the back of the bow to lock your fingers against, while holding your pencil rigid between your thumb and forefinger. With a little practice, an even taper can be easily achieved. Whichever method you employ, draw the taper on both sides of your bow, as most of us tend to lean towards the pencil line with the cutting tool. At least if the line is on both sides of the bow, you should end up with the flat, tapered, square profile that we are hoping to achieve throughout the length of the limbs.

After this stage, you should have a fully tapered, rectangular cross-section longbow, with each side perpendicular to the next. Before we go any further, it is worth spending some time cleaning up the back of the bow. Sand it down as smoothly as possible, perhaps even rubbing it over with a stone to really crush down those fibres. This reduces the chance of any of those fibres lifting when the bow is bent. You're aiming to create a surface that is so smooth that it is difficult for a fault to start.

At this stage, it is also worth rounding the corners of the back of the bow: this will reduce splintering when the bow is handled or in transit. It is very disappointing to finish your bow, only to have a splinter rip right across the back surface, creating the possibility of more lifting fibres. How far you round the corners is somewhat a matter of taste or a question of how many bad mistakes you need to cover up from your initial roughing out. It could be as simple as running over the edges with a cabinet scraper or some sandpaper, or you might have to match any damage that was caused by using a heavier tool.

close-up of the D-section of a longbow.

Now you need to think about putting the D-section of the longbow in place. To do this, establish a second centre line, this time on the belly of the bow. This centre line should allow us to remove wood evenly from both sides of the limb. If you don't take this precaution and end up taking more wood from one side than the other, your bow is likely to twist in the direction where there is less wood.

However, prior to this, have a good look at your bow. Is the taper as even as possible? Can you see any hills on the surface of the wood? Those will be stiff spots. Can you see any valleys? They're weak spots. These will show up at some later stage in the bow-making process, so it is much wiser to deal with them now. If your carpentry has been good, then the tillering process – the real heart of bow-making – is vastly speeded up and simplified.

Happy? Good. Now the centre line is in place, we can start knocking the corners of the belly off. Start by creating half an octagon. This leaves ridges or ribs that, in turn, you can remove and undercut. The process is quite difficult to explain: you should be trying to move the tool over the whole surface of the bow evenly, creating facets and knocking them down again, until you're left with that nice half-circle profile. Ideally, your half-circle should be quite flattened – think of it as a D-shape.

It's quite easy to make the bow peak in the middle, which is known as leaving it 'high-arched'. This puts considerable compression force on a comparatively narrow area. (Perhaps 'galleon-shaped' is a better way of describing how your finished D-section should look: like the shallow draft of a boat.)

Once the D-section is complete, you can move on to the next stage: tillering. (This is covered after the section on flatbows.)

Flatbows

Even if you have no intention of building a longbow, do have a good look at the preceding section before you get stuck in here. Many of the criteria – in terms of roughing out, timber selection and so on – apply every bit as much to crafting a flatbow as they do to making longbows. The only real differences between flatbows and longbows at this stage are the dimensions that you rough out – and, as you'll discover later in this chapter, the tillering process.

Dimensions

Over the following pages I describe two of my favourite flatbow designs: the Holmegaard, which is a very robust, drag-through-the-woods type of bow; and the Mollegabet, which demands slightly more advanced carpentry skills to produce what is arguably the fastest-shooting, all-wood bow possible. These are two of the oldest designs found in Europe, with the earliest examples dating back some 8,000 years.

When making a flatbow, there is no tradition of shortening the lower limb. This means that when we are marking out, even though we are still allowing a 4in (10cm) handle, it will have to be placed in the exact centre of the stave. As previously suggested, for flatbow designs, the minimum length of the stave should be 68in (1.72m). For some of these designs a full 6ft (1.82m) would not be excessive for a first attempt.

As is true for the longbow, the only real downside of making the limbs of your bow longer is that it adds mass, which reduces mechanical efficiency. However, again, the trade-off is that force applied over longer limbs means less chance of breakages, compression frets and all sorts of other nasty things that we will discuss in the tillering section below.

Marking Out the Flatbow

In terms of laying out, the handles for each of these designs are the same.

- Measure out your handle to 4in x 1in (10cm x 25mm) – it is fine to make this grip longer (some designs suggest 5 or even 6in (12.5–15cm) in length, but to my mind this is excessive unless you have huge hands).

- All you need is enough room for your hand and for the arrow to be able to sit on top of your hand in a position that ensures it passes the narrowest part of the bow.

- Measure this from a centre line established in the same way as described above for the longbow.

- Above the handle, taper a fade or fishtail from the 1in (25mm)-wide handle section to the final width of the limb.

- This limb width will vary according to the timber used: high-density woods such as yew or hawthorn can be made much narrower, perhaps as thin as 1½in (37mm), while lower-density timber such as ash would be better left 1¾in (42mm) wide as a minimum.

Of course, your decision about limb width will also depend on the design – not least the intended draw weight of the bow. We are still bound by basic physics, so if we want to make a bow that is much more powerful but are using low-density wood, it will have to be wider and/or longer. Although they can be made in heavy weights, I think these flatbow designs create much more elegant weapons when kept at low hunting weights – 50lb (22.6kg) is plenty. (At those weights, the dimensions I've described are a good starting point. Rather than confuse by trying to specify more complicated measurements in words, please refer to the illustrations on p144–5.)

Holmegaard Versus Mollegabet Flatbow

In general terms, there are a few points to consider regarding the pros and cons of these two different flatbow designs.

155

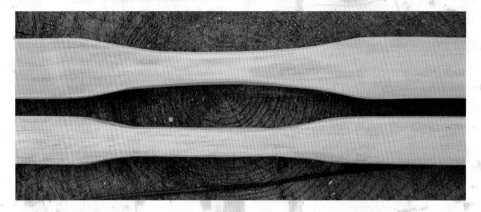

A flatbow handle and fade detail.

The top profiles of a Holmegaard (top) and Mollegabet (bottom).

The side view of Mollegabet, second fade.

The plan view a Mollegabet, second fade.

Holmegaard Bow

The Holmegaard bow stays the same width from the handle to at least the halfway point – even slightly past it – then narrows abruptly to the limb tips. Exactly where this begins is open to interpretation, but the closer to the handle, the less working limb there is – therefore, the more strain that limb is under. Reducing the size of the limb tips has the effect of reducing mass at the very ends, exactly where it should be light. The wide working part reinforces the bow at the point of greatest strain.

Mollegabet Bow

The Mollegabet bow is a highly tuned-up Holmegaard, with the limbs made extremely light and stiff. It is this low mass that, as mentioned previously, makes the Mollegabet arguably the fastest-shooting, straight-stave, all-wood bow possible. The downside of the design is that greater strain is placed on the working part: the limb. This effect is because the working part is very much shortened by the non-bending tips, also, the need for a second fade or fishtail to reinforce the extreme narrowing of the limb tip. However, while the carpentry here is quite complex, the tillering is usually faster, as only the much shorter working part of the limb needs attention.

Tillering

Here we come to the heart of the bow-making process. All your hard work so far has been tree felling and carpentry, now it gets complicated!

Some kind of tillering jig will be needed, although it is possible to do this whole process using a mirror. Tillers come in a variety of designs, but my preference is for the set-up illustrated here. It uses a pulley wheel and a hook, which allows me to gently flex and release the bow, helping the fibres to get orientated. I dislike tillers that hold the bow drawn for long periods of time.

In my opinion, tillering is a four-part process, with every element as important as the next.

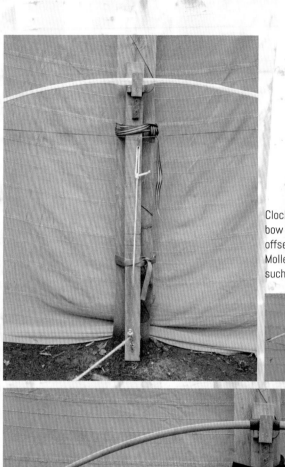

Clockwise from below: A longbow with offset handle: this bow bends through its handle; A longbow with stiffened offset handle; A Holmegaard-style bow in a tiller; A Mollegabet bow reflexed on one side. Tillers with pulleys such as this are kinder on wood fibres.

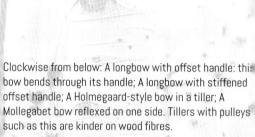

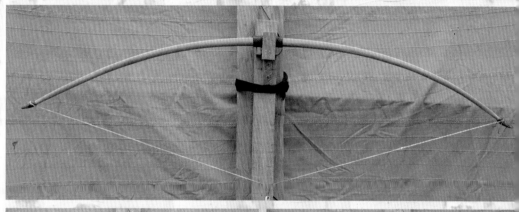

1. Side Profile

Achieving the correct side profile for the design of the bow essentially means making sure that, when the bow is bent, each limb balances and forms the arc of curve most appropriate to its design. Each design described has a slightly different side profile. To take them in turn, they should look roughly as follows.

First, for a longbow that bends through the handle – as is traditional– and made with an offset handle – also traditional – the side profile starting from the centre of the bow is flattened slightly. Despite bending in the handle, it docsn't follow the arc of a circle through the handle; the handle area is slightly stiff. From the end of this slightly stiffened section, the limb should gently curve, with the entire limb working evenly. This means no stiff spots. At approximately 8–10in (20–25cm) from the end, the limb tips should appear unbending.

Should you have chosen to make a centre-shot longbow, each limb should look exactly the same. With an off-centre longbow, the lower limb will appear slightly shorter and stiffer than the upper limb. This is quite subtle, and generally needs pointing out to the novice to be recognised. If the centre of the bow is stiffened, the same profile will apply, except this time the centre of the handle will appear flat and stiffer for a longer distance. This is the case for the example illustrated.

For the Mollegabet and Holmegaard bows, the limbs start to work immediately from the fades. They stop bending at the second fade, then appear stiff right the way down to the tip. With the Mollegabet, this is more extreme, and in practice it is sometimes advisable to let these long, stiff levers bend a little bit, just to take some pressure off the main working part of the limb.

The one illustrated below has a reflex in one of its limbs, but not in the other. This has the effect of making the bend look a little uneven.

2. Training the Fibres

This is crucial, but neither well described nor sufficiently emphasised in many accounts of bow-making. If you rough out the perfect bow, tie a string to it and pull it back to the length of the arrow, you're quite likely to be disappointed by the result. It is very important throughout the tillering process that the bow is flexed sufficiently and gently enough to orientate the fibres to being bent in a specific way. This is also particularly important when removing wood to correct faults.

Imagine your bow has been slightly bent on the tiller. The back of the bow is under tension, the belly is under compression, and somewhere between the two is an area of wood that's neither in tension nor compression – or it's in both (which is a concept I have never quite understood). This area is termed 'the neutral axis'.

As we correct faults, trying to achieve a good side profile, we remove wood from the belly side of the bow. This exposes fibres that may have previously been in tension to compression forces, and vice versa. This can be damaging and may even break the bow. Aside from averting a major disaster, it is important to allow these fibres time to become orientated to their new forces, just to be certain that your changes have come into effect.

For example, if there is a stiff spot in one of the bow's limbs, removal of wood at that point should weaken the area. However, if we merely bend the bow a couple of times after making the correction, it could be that nothing will change in the stiffened area, simply because the fibres have not had a chance to change. This may well lead to removal of too much wood, with unfortunate results.

Training the wood in this way also reduces the likelihood of creating compression frets (as explained shortly on p.161).

3. Draw Weight
Arriving at the right draw weight is critical, as there is absolutely no point in building a beautiful bow with a perfect side profile, then giving yourself a double hernia every time you try to shoot it! This is avoided relatively easily by never taking the bow further than its intended finished draw weight.

4. Draw Length
The previous three elements – a well-trained bow with its fibres all orientated correctly, a side profile that looks exactly as it should for its design, and a draw weight that can be managed – must all happen at the draw length that is suited to the bow's owner. This does vary a little between individuals of different sizes and physical prowess, but for most people, somewhere between 26 and 29in (66–74cm) will be about right. This effectively equates to the length of your arrow.

The Process

To begin the tillering process, you will need some non-stretching string, so it might well be worth jumping ahead to the next section on string-making before you read any more. The earlier stages of bow-making can be done with parachute cord (paracord), but this gives a false indication when you are tillering, especially of the draw weight, because it stretches.

In addition, you will need to cut tillering nocks, which can be permanent or greatly reduced to lighten the limb tips further, making the bow even more efficient. Ensure the nocks are pointing the right way and there is a deep enough shoulder to hold the string without danger. (A detailed description of how to do this, with accompanying photographs, is in the string nocks section on p.164.)

If you have made a string, place its loop on the top limb – it is a good idea at this stage to decide on an upper and a lower limb, even for a centre-shot bow. This is to avoid suddenly pulling fibres in a direction to which they are not orientated. In traditional archery, the top limb is the one with the loop, while the bottom limb has the knot. Getting into this habit early also ensures that when shooting the finished bow, you don't inadvertently hold it upside down. So long as the loop is uppermost, you should be safe. The knot used on the lower limb is a timber hitch (about which more in Chapter 9).

When I first started making bows, I would generally make a reasonable bow with a good side profile and then worry about how heavy it was. So, I would then have to spend ages taking off more wood, until I could manage to shoot it. This often works fine if you're dealing with dense tropical hardwoods. However, when making bows from more delicate timbers, you need to take a slightly more subtle approach, lest you seriously damage the bow or even break it. For the next section, I have borrowed shamelessly from some American research that came out over the last twenty or so years – check out *The Traditional Bowyer's Bible* series for more information.

This suggests that, to avoid overstraining the bow and potentially damaging it, you should never push it further than its intended finished draw weight. In practice, this means that if the bow is intended to weigh 50lb (22.6kg), then each time the bow is bent, it goes no further – or at least is pulled no harder – than 50lb. If the limbs are drawn down to a 6in (15cm) tip deflection and the weight hits 50lb, stop pulling. Check the side profile and all the other elements that are part of tillering. If all is in order, make the bow lighter by the even removal of wood. This process is repeated until the bow hits the required draw length, hopefully at exactly its desired weight.

How this works is fairly straightforward – albeit a little bit tedious – until you gain some experience of building bows. It takes a little while to understand how much effect a certain amount of work will have on the issue that you are trying to correct, which can add up to a lot of patient tweaking.

Before you start the tillering process, check the bow to see if there are any obvious lumps or bumps across its surface. If a bow has significant hills and valleys, it will affect the curve. It is likely to be too stiff in the hills and too weak in the valleys. In fact, as I mentioned above, with a longbow it is worth checking this before it is D-sectioned, because hills and valleys are easier to see when the back, belly and sides are at right angles to each other.

To reiterate, it is also worth making sure the bow's back is pristine. This is the part of the bow that could potentially lift at damaged areas or toolmarks. Remember to round the corners at the back of the bow at this point, too. An additional advantage of taking care before tillering begins is that when the bow is finished, it should be at its correct weight – it is quite easy to finish a bow at 50lb, then find yourself losing a fair bit just from sanding.

- Put the string very loose on the bow. Place the bow on the tiller, with its handle central to the tiller post.

- Attach the hook to the string and flex it gently. Remember that your bow is a piece of wood that has never been bent before so, at this early stage, great care must be taken not to overstrain – or even break – the bow. Perhaps twenty or thirty gentle bounces should see the bow warmed up and give you an indication as to whether it is bending evenly or not.

- At this point, a scale can be incorporated into the tiller rope, to avoid pulling the bow past its intended draw weight.

- Should the tiller shape look correct, having avoided the common problems outlined below, carry on, gently deflecting the tips a little more each time.

- If through this extra effort and movement in the bow limbs, the draw weight goes over the intended target, remove wood evenly across the whole of the bow, particularly the working parts, blending into the tips and handles so as not to create steps. It is important to avoid working one limb more than the other at this point, otherwise you'll lose the perfect curve that is needed.

- Once this has been achieved and the string has hit the 16 or 18in (40–45cm) mark on the tiller, it is time to brace the bow slightly. A brace height describes the distance between the belly of the bow and the bowstring when the string is tight. (I discuss the pros and cons of different brace heights later in this chapter, on p.170.)

- For now, we need to shorten the string and brace the bow with the string tight and perhaps 2in (50mm) distant from the belly.

- Do lots of warming and bouncing on the tiller before and after this, checking the curve and the draw weight as you go along.

- Should all be well, continue to increase the brace until it is around 6in (15cm) from the belly of the bow. (You need to measure from the centre of the wood: don't measure from the raised handle of a flatbow.)

- Now, check the weight throughout, and gradually bring the bow back to the required draw length, correcting as needed.

I would encourage you, by this point, to be using fairly fine tools to do any corrections – unless of course you put your bow on the tiller and it weighs 178lb (80kg). In such a case, you might want to have at it with a spoke shave.

In the early stages, it's good to keep a few spare pounds in hand to allow for corrections. If, for example, in the first stages your bow is weighing around 60lb (27kg), then you have 10lb (4.5kg) to lose while you correct any faults. So, scrapers and rasps are likely to be the order of the day, to avoid overcooking your corrections and ending up with a child's bow. (Incidentally, this is also where the bowyer's life can get very frustrating.)

String Nocks

Making string nocks is a relatively simple affair, with a round rasp or file making the ideal tool for the job. All of the bows described in this chapter are, at their tips, ½in x ½in (12 x 12mm).

Measure from the tip down a further ½in (12mm), then yet another, and draw this square around the sides of the bow limb. Because of the almost square nature of the tips, bisecting this square corner-to-corner gives an almost 45° angle – ideal for filing in the grooves.

It is important not to file too deeply across the back of the bow, but this must be balanced with providing enough of a 'shoulder' for the string to sit in the nock securely. If made too shallow, the string may break out and take some of the bow with it. These types of nocks can be replaced later, as shown below, or kept permanently.

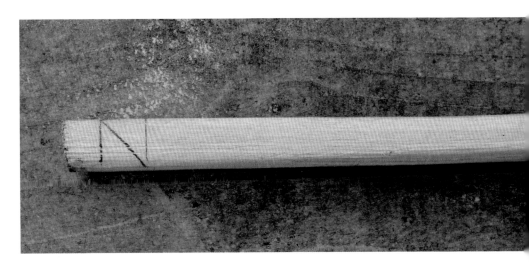

String nocks.

ring nocks.

Common Problems with Tillering

Tillering is something that is much easier to grasp from doing rather than reading about it. However, I will outline some of the common problems likely to occur during the process.

Hinges

It must be said that while hinges are a great help in opening doors and felling trees, they are also pretty bad when it comes to bow-making. They are the areas of the bow that bend significantly more than anywhere else, hence the name. To deal with a hinge effectively, it must be spotted early. If a hinge goes unnoticed, your bow is likely to be significantly weakened at this point and may never form a smooth arc.

The treatment is to weaken areas either side of the excessive bend point. Once a hinge has been spotted, all other work should be stopped until the problem is cured. Continuing to pull down on the stave after hinges have been noted is likely to make them permanent.

A hinge example.

This Moaro Health bow is so uneven, I dare not pull it back too far.

Uneven Tiller

It's entirely possible to have two perfectly good curves, describing the exact arc for your bow design, but where one limb is bending significantly more than the other. If not corrected, the unevenness of the strain may cause the bow to break. To cure this, wood should be removed evenly across the working part of the stiffer limb until it begins to match its mate.

Weakness in the Handle

This is how I describe excessive bending in the handle area, which causes the main part of the bow limb to appear stiff, like wings that have suddenly collapsed. It's a common cause of problems among beginners, usually due to a temptation to remove wood in the handle area because it does not appear to be bending.

Think of how the bow works: first the outer limbs bend, to be followed by the rest of the limb, which should work evenly into the handle. In the early stages of tillering, because the bow limbs have not been pulled down far enough to work into the handle, the handle may appear stiffer than it is.

Removal of wood at this point may come back to haunt the bow-maker. It may well be that when the centre section of the bow does finally come into play, so much wood has been removed that it collapses at this point. In reality, it is quite hard to do this, so long as the possibility is kept in mind – which is why I don't have the most extreme illustration of it. However, from the fades, the bow limbs bend barely at all, right down to the tips.

Not the most extreme example, but this bow has excessive near-handle bend, especially in the left limb.

Whip-Ended

A bow is said to be whip-ended when there is very little movement through the centre section, and most of the work is instead being done by the bow ends. In the best-case scenario, the bow is merely inefficient, with very little wood doing any work, and the bow therefore storing little energy.

In more severe cases, the bow may hinge at the bend point, develop frets or break. A whip can occur at any point along the working limb or on one limb only.

To deal with this issue, first identify the point where the bend starts and remove wood on the handle side, just above this bend point. Work in 2–3in (5–7cm) increments, removing wood to chase the bend back into the handle, using the draw weight of the bow as a guide. To chase the bend back into the handle, working from the outside is vital to avoid creating a weakness in the handle.

! 1. There is no point drawing a bow further if you can spot a fault at brace.
2. This tiller profile does not improve by drawing back further.

Damaging Your Bow

I've talked a lot about pushing the bow too hard and the potential for damage. This damage manifests itself along a scale of severity, with the highest being a broken bow. The next in line are compression frets: these look like little jagged tool marks running across the belly of the bow, with the key difference being that sanding them out doesn't remove them, it just chases them deeper into the bow.

These frets are areas where the wood has taken a strain that it can't support and collapsed. Invariably, this creates huge weak points – in the best-case scenario they may stay for years, merely making the bow inefficient; the worst-case scenario is that the bow breaks at these points.

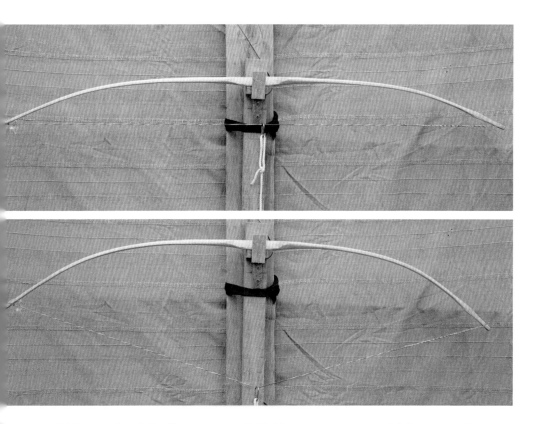

There is no point drawing a bow further if you can spot a fault at brace – as you can see, this bow does not improve.

Compression frets.

String Follow

This is just a reminder, as this is a slightly less serious, but no less energy-robbing, scenario. It reveals itself when the bow appears strung when not braced. Part of the efficiency of the bow, or at least the energy stored in it that is available to the arrow, comes from how hard you make the bow limbs work, as previously described. Bows with excessive string follow store less energy.

Solving Tiller Faults

These images illustrate a few tiller faults and possible solutions.

Brace Height

Achieving the correct brace height is something worth experimenting with. While there are brace heights that are evidently too high or too low, many archers adjust the distance to suit their individual shooting style, or even individual bows. Personally, I suggest as a minimum that the fletching can clear the bow with the bow at rest.

There are a couple of things of which to be aware. If the brace is too high, then the bow is under greater strain but is not storing more energy than a bow with a lower brace. For example, if a bow is braced to 8in (20cm) and the archer has a 28in (71cm) draw, then the archer can make the bow move 20in (50cm). Put another way, the bow stores 20in (50cm)

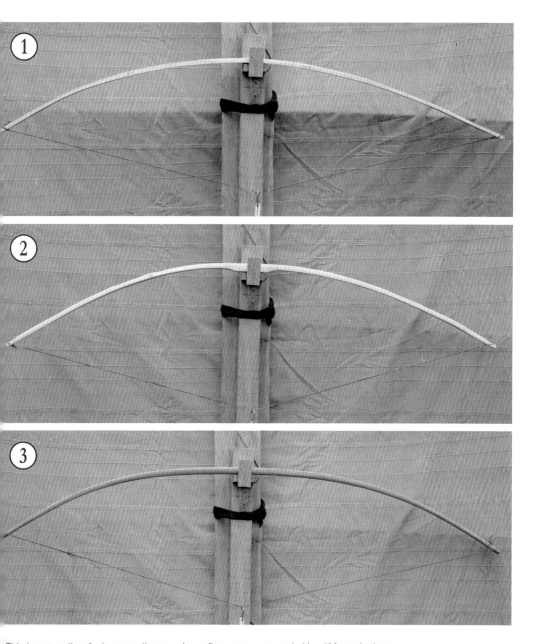

This is not really a fault: naturally occurring reflex may never unwind itself from the bow.

This red oak Holmegaard bow is too stiff on the right-hand limb, near to the handle. Gentle wood removal is required. This is the bow illustrated on p.156, with its fault corrected.

This bow is too stiff in the handle section. The secret to correcting these faults is to find the point of stiffness and remove wood to chase the bend back into the handle.

worth of energy. If the same archer braces a bow at 6in (15cm), the bow is now travelling 22in (55cm) and thus storing more energy.

There are downsides to a low brace. First, even wearing a bracer won't protect you from the string slapping your wrist and raising a painful welt. Second, the archer's paradox: this is the action of the arrow bending, or paradoxing, around the bow then straightening out. This oscillation from bend to straight again is important for accurate shooting.

Arrows are matched to the bow using the draw weight as a guide and need to be sufficiently stiff to bend and then straighten out. With traditional archery, the hand holding the bow becomes the arrow rest, and sits against the side of the bow. If the arrows are too stiff, they tend to fly left or right, depending on the handedness of the archer. If they are too soft, they may well wobble all the way to the target. This arrow stiffness is expressed as 'spine'. Even with the best-matched arrows, a very low brace height pushes the arrow forcefully into the belly of the bow and causes severe paradox. Brace height can be individual to both the archer and a particular bow and is something with which you should experiment.

Limb Tips

Once the bow is finished in terms of being in tiller, it is worthwhile look-ing at the limb tips and making them as light as possible. It quite easy to become extremely nervous at this point, with breakage paranoia creeping in. If it is impossible to shake this feeling, feel free to leave the bow limbs as they are. Performance will be lost, but for a beginner, who cares?

It might be of some comfort to hold on to the thought that bow limbs should be stiff and unbending, but wood must bend before it can break. Unless the bow has been made excessively heavy in the limb tips, then most of the lightening work is likely to involve taking wood from the sides.

If done correctly, glued-on pieces of horn or wood may have to be used, as the tips are so light and slender there is now no room left for filed string groves. Traditionally, longbows had horn nocks covering the whole of the bow tip, mainly, I think, because heavy bows of yew suffer from the string biting into the timber. To fit these efficiently, a ½in (12mm) taper drill is needed to hollow out the horn, and the limb tip needs to be shaped into a cone to marry up with the horn. These tips can be as simple or elaborate as required. (I prefer simplicity and keep horn nocks as light and unadorned as possible.) Both nock options need to finish with their bases flush to the bow stave. Any lip left on the nock will make stringing the bow very awkward.

Finishing

Finishing is a matter of preference to a large extent. Some prefer oils, while others prefer varnish. What is important is that the finished surface should be as smooth as possible, to reduce the likelihood of a fault starting – working on the principle that a big splinter starts from a small one. It is also important that the surface beads water.

I like to finish with oil and then wax, only after a severe and vigorous sanding and the application of several coats of boiled linseed oil. Mixed initially with white spirit, at a ratio of 70 per cent white spirit to 30 per cent oil, this is followed by a 50/50 mix, again for several coats, and finally a finish with 100 per cent oil. (I believe, rightly or wrongly, that the white spirit helps the oil to penetrate.)

Opposite: Various string nocks can be made to suit individual tastes.

Various handles can be
added to your bow –
leather or cord, or nothir
at all. The cord handle ha
a leather strip underneat
to bulk up the grip, and t
one with no wrap shows
an arrow plate of horn.

Finally, I rub in either pure beeswax or an old-fashioned furniture wax that is high in both wax and linseed. Normally I finish by boning: odd as it sounds, the bow can be worked with a smooth pebble, glass bottle or indeed, a bone. This has the effect of really closing the grain down and making the wood impressively smooth. Aside from the principle that a fault needs a starting point, the need to find elegance in your craft means that it is impossible to do too much finishing.

Handles

Medieval longbows had no handle wrap: they came as unadorned as possible, in a typical army-issue way. This is not to say that they cannot be adorned with anything you care to try, including leather, bark or decorative cord. It is also worth considering an arrow plate, which sits on the side of the bow and protects the wood from the arrow wearing a groove in it. Once again, this was something that war bows didn't have; instead, they bore the mark of the bowyer, which essentially told the archer where the arrow passed, and therefore where to hold the bow.

I think arrow plates finish a bow off. I normally make mine with a sliver of horn, although mother of pearl, seashells, hardwood, antler or bone can be, and have all been, used.

Chisel a small relief in the side of the bow, glue in the insert and abrade it flush to the surrounding wood. All sorts of funky shapes can be made, depending on your level of skill and creativity.

Bowstrings

String-Making

String-making, like many practical tasks, is easier to describe with images rather than words, so I have included lots here. The materials vary widely: it is possible to make a bowstring from bark, nettles, linen and a host of other natural materials. However, for your first bow – and especially for tillering – I would use an over-long (and maybe over-strong) string. It might even be wise to purchase something modern to do the job for you, although for the purist, linen can be bought quite easily (this was the material of choice for medieval bows).

The key factor is that the string should be relatively low-stretch, to make the wood of the bow do the work. Excessive string stretch drastically reduces the efficiency of a bow – it isn't a catapult. Excessive string weight can also slow down a bow's performance.

The following explanation is one of the simplest methods of making a decent bowstring. The elements can then be elaborated on, as will be explained at the end. I am assuming the use of Dacron B50 or B55 string. There are many modern alternatives, but I have used this for many years, and it is cheap and easy to come by. For around half the price of buying a made bowstring, it is possible to purchase enough Dacron for a dozen – that said, you may consider the higher price worth paying, after having tried out this next process. Dacron has some stretch, but many regard this as important to cushion the forces when the arrow leaves the bow. There are almost entirely non-stretch strings available, but I have never felt the need to use them.

The following description is for a bowstring with a laid-in loop: that is, a loop effectively spliced into the string permanently. A loop is stronger than a knot and makes sliding the string over the top nock much simpler than trying to tie a knot, as you must with the lower limb, where a timber hitch is used to secure the string. I like this arrangement better than doubled, looped strings, as it allows infinite adjustment of the brace height by merely tightening or loosening the knot.

The number of strands in a string depends very much on how powerful the bow is and the material used. For the bows made using the dimensions provided, twelve strands should be enough. If using linen, this should be increased depending on the linen strand diameter.

- Start with two pegs, set around 18in (45cm) longer than the bow itself. You can bang stakes into the ground or use clamps – the choice is yours.

- Run out twelve strands over this distance and split them into two bundles of six. These bundles should be hanked, as shown, and secured with a half-hitch to allow them to spin. (For knots and ropework, see Chapter 9.)

- You will need a reasonably long tail on these bundles, first to form the eye of the loop, and then to fold over to form the splice. The length of splice is important, as it is secured by friction – too short, and it will pull out.

The following comments mark another real eureka moment for me. When I first started making strings, it was before the age of the internet, so finding good information was quite tricky. I tried splicing and twisting and generally fiddling about until a single photo in a book gave me the inspiration I needed to work it out. (Before continuing, it may be useful to read the section in Chapter 5 on cordage making.)

Assuming you have two hanked bundles as illustrated, the process is very similar to making normal cordage. However, ordinarily a bundle of fibres would be clamped in one hand and twisted in the other, until pushing one hand towards the next creates a kink in the fibres. This kink is encouraged to wrap around itself, giving both a small section of finished cordage and two strands. When making a bowstring, we are already starting with two strands, and so miss out the initial kink.

- Bearing this in mind, begin making cordage by clamping the two strands and twisting (as described in Chapter 5). Because we are lacking the initial kink, it may be difficult at first to prevent the cordage from unwinding itself.

- If this happens, merely turn the cordage around and start making more of it, going back in the other direction. The starting point is quite critical here. We need to start far enough up from the ends of the strands so that there is enough material to fold over and form the spliced loop.

- Stagger each strand, so that they do not run out at the same time. Using this technique, make enough cordage to form the loop, which needs to fit over your bow and slide down.

The bowstring is always kept on the bow, which can be seen clearly in the image overleaf describing stringing. This illustrates the need for the string to slide down the bow limb to some extent.

- Once you have made a couple of inches of cordage, fold this over into a loop, leaving two short-fibre bundles and two long-fibre bundles.

- At this stage, wrap the bundles of short fibres around the bundles of long fibres and carry on twisting, this time clamping at the base of the loop and forming an eye splice.

- Continue making cordage until an inch or so past the longest bundle.

- There is no need to make cordage the full length of the string. At this point, the loop can be hooked over a convenient post and the remaining fibres loosely wrapped around themselves. Modern Dacron is pre-waxed, but you may wish to add wax at this stage.

- More cordage can be made at the other end, where the string is attached to the bottom limb using a timber hitch. This end cordage, while not strictly needed, does make tying the hitch much easier, neater and less likely to abrade.

- Finish with a simple overhand knot. Generally, the timber hitch is never untied and remains permanently on the bow.

This simple string can be embellished to make an even finer product. For example, the string can be twisted from three bundles of fibres instead of two. Extra strands can be incorporated at the loop to reinforce this most-used area. (There was a point during my courses when I stopped teaching the elaboration, as I found myself making so many strings for my students. I think from a learning perspective, it is much preferable to learn the basic method and then elaborate yourself.)

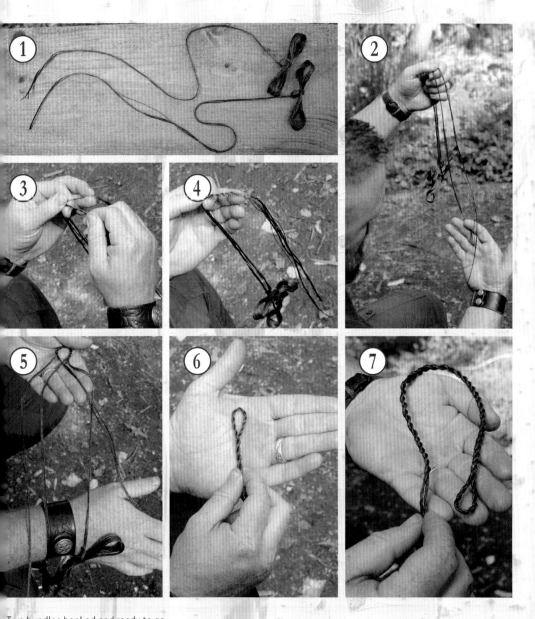

Two bundles hanked and ready to go.

Pinch the bundle together leaving a slight overlap.

Start 10in (25cm) from the end of the bundles.

Make a short length of cordage, enough to form a loop that will slide over the bow tip.

Fold the cordage over to form a loop and combine the short lengths with the coiled long lengths.

Continue to make cord, this time twisting the short and long fibres together.

Carry on until 2in (5cm) past the point where the short fibres become buried in the lay.

Hold the bow at the handle, bracing its lower limb against your foot. Pull in at the handle, while at the same time using the heel of the other hand to push the limb tip down. Slide the loop up into the string grooves.

To destring, have the belly of the bow facing you and pull the limb tip while pushing in the handle. The thumb and forefinger should be able to lift the loop free.

How to String

There are three methods for stringing a bow, but only two of them are recommended. Stringing needs to be done in such a way that each limb of your bow is bent equally.

Serving

Serving the centre of the string is essential to protect the strands from wear and even breakage caused by the nock of the arrow and, to a lesser extent, the archer's fingers. Specialist serving thread is available, but silk, linen and even dental floss serve just as well. The material chosen just needs to be tough.

Serving is best done on the bow with the bow braced to its full height, as this gives a true indication of the central position. Shortening and lengthening the brace height is done by shortening and lengthening the string, moving the centre position each time. There needs to be enough of the string served to accommodate three fingers of the archer, plus the arrow, plus a couple of inches for adjustments.

Seriously consider buying a serving tool. They are relatively cheap and allow adjustment, which makes it very easy to get the tension right; it is quite fiddly just to use thread on a reel.

vill be useful to clamp the bow down to apply the serving.

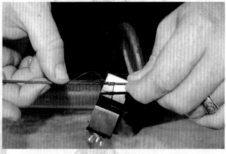

Lay a loop across the bowstring and wrap it up perhaps half a dozen times, capturing the loop against the string.

Pull the tail end of the loop away and continue wrapping. The tail end can now be yanked tight.

The captured loop.

Above: Tension your serving tool and continue down the string until you are happy with the amount of serving produced. The serving thread can now be cut free of the spool but be sure to leave a generous tail to finish off.

Left: Wrap a further six or eight times around a pencil or arrow shaft, and then thread the tail end of the serving through these loops. It gets slightly fiddly here, as the pencil will need to be pulled out and the whole thing tensioned by pulling on the end of the serving thread. This can be difficult to achieve without making a bird's nest

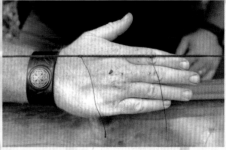

Now the ends can be trimmed off and perhaps a dab of superglue applied, just for security.

A served string.

Arrows

Length and Weight

It is important to have a good idea of the length that the arrow needs to be, which is best assessed by working out your draw length. When working this out, bear in mind that the arm holding the bow should be slightly bent, thus shortening the draw. Modern bows allow the archer to hyperextend the elbow joint, which is not a good idea in any sport, and certainly not with a traditional bow of any kind of weight. Most of us will shoot around the 26–28in (65–70cm) mark so, when looking for arrow shafts, somewhere around 30in (75cm) is a good start.

Commercially available arrow shafts can be found quite easily, which may be the best route to take. Making a decent arrow is quite complicated, and making a matching set even more so. I have mentioned already the archer's paradox, which means that all your arrows should match the draw weight of your bow.

Commercially available arrows are graded in 5lb (2.3kg) increments – 30–35lb, 35–40lb and so on – but this figure is only a starting point. It is not as simple as having a 50lb (22.6kg) draw-weight bow and buying 50lb spine arrow shafts. A longbow with a fairly wide handle may need arrows slightly softer, in order to allow the shaft to bend around the bow. Making arrows longer has the effect of softening the spine, while making them shorter stiffens it. A heavy point also softens the spine and may require a stronger shaft.

For consistent shooting, all your arrows should be – at least in theory – of consistent physical weight. Generally, manufactured arrows are made from boards that are sawn down to squares. These squares then have their corners knocked off, turning them into hexagons, the edges of which can be either turned into further multisided shapes or rounded, depending on the equipment available.

It is possible to do this in the home workshop with hand tools. A V-shaped trough can be cut into a board, with a stop at the end. The squared blank then can be laid in this slot to allow the edges to be knocked off to the point where a cabinet scraper and sandpaper can finish the job. The starting square would have to be sufficient to leave enough wood to make your arrow shafts the correct and consistent diameter.

Testing the Arrow

After all this, you will still need to test the arrow spines for consistency. In modern times, funky machines known as 'spine testers' have been created: these work by balancing the arrow shafts across consistent centres. A weight is then hung from the centre and the amount of flex in the shaft measured by the movement of a needle that is linked to the shaft and/or weight. Ideally, the shafts are tested in two planes by turning the arrow. These spine testers are expensive to buy, but clever mathematical and engineering types could probably make their own. (Of course, the tester would need calibrating to be accurate.)

Having said all of this, it is possible to make arrows from arrow-like sticks found in the woods and hedgerows, and to do it without worrying too much about a spine tester. In many ways, this is a logical step, since our ancestors must have managed to make weapons accurate enough for hunting without any extra contraptions, because otherwise we wouldn't be here.

The issues and exaggerations in arrow flight are more pronounced the further the arrow travels. It is possible to get away with a lot more if you are shooting relatively short distances, perhaps recreating hunting as opposed to target shooting over longer distances, but that isn't to suggest that woods-made arrows couldn't hit a target regularly at longer distances.

There are alternatives to spine testers that I tentatively suggest our ancestors may have used. The first – and most obvious – is to make a bunch of arrows as similar as possible, shoot them all a few times, and reject the ones that wobble or go shooting off to the side. (Incidentally, it is not unheard of for modern archers to shoot and reject manufactured wooden arrows in the same way, although with modern materials it is much easier to arrive at perfectly matched arrows.)

In the beginning, of course, arrows flying off to the side may well be due to bad shooting and the best-made arrows in the world can't help with that. Stiff arrows are easier to deal with, in that more wood can be carefully removed from the length of the shaft until they loosen up a bit. (I also believe that, with experience, it is possible to judge with some accuracy the spine of an arrow by flexing it.)

It is possible to buy shafts singly these days, so getting two or three around the draw weight that you think you need could be a good investment. Flexing these, then flexing your own-made shafts as a comparison and removing wood as needed, is a great way to get into the ballpark.

After a while, a good sense of the suitability of an arrow shaft can be gained without needing the shop-bought yardsticks.

On top of this, if the arrows are all the same weight, accuracy is likely to be further improved, although I don't think this is as important as spine unless the weight differences are extreme. If you want to be super-accurate, small scales can be bought relatively cheaply. Harvesting the same species of tree from the same location is also likely to give shafts a similar wood density, and therefore weight and spine.

Width

Before we talk about the mechanics of making arrows, it is worth having a few things fixed in your mind, including how thick you want to make them. This will be governed to some extent by the material available, but also by the weight of the bow in general terms. If you are making huge, knight-slaying war arrows, thicker shafts will be needed to get close to a suitable spine. There is evidence that while many medieval arrows were made from worked-down timber, some were also from small-diameter roundwood. Often, such arrows are called 'self-arrows', just as bows hewn from a tree that use no backing or other materials are called 'self-bows'. (More on self-arrows in the next section.)

Commercially, arrows are available in several diameters, depending on their spine. The lower spine shafts start at around 5/16in (7.9mm), then change to 11/32in (8.7mm) as they begin to need more wood to retain spine. Heavy-bow shooters go further than this to 3/8in (9.5mm), then everything mysteriously changes from imperial to metric and shafts become available in measurements such as 12mm. (I tend towards buying the component parts and assembling them, since I shoot mostly in the woods and therefore lose a fair few arrows. It is easier and less time-consuming to replace arrows made in this way.)

Whether you choose modern or primitive shafts, the basic principles are the same.

- Cut a nock in the end of the arrow shaft to accept the string. The simplest way to do this is to cut two opposing V-notches, about an inch from the end of the arrow shaft. The distance between the points of these two notches gives the diameter of the nock.

- About ¼in (6mm) below these cuts, and on the opposite side, make the horizontal stop cut.

- Next, place a knife firmly in the base of the 'V' and twist. This should split the wood down until it hits the stop cuts. However, do not rely on these stops, and instead reinforce with your thumb. (This looks much more dangerous than it is, as you are not actually carving towards yourself, merely twisting the knife.)

- Once this has been done in both 'V' cuts, the head of the shaft can be rocked backwards and forwards until the arrow nock breaks out and is revealed.

There are a couple of additional points to consider. First, it is important that the string is a snug fit in the arrow nock, to the point where it should hang on the string without falling. If not, there is a strong possibility that the arrow release when shooting will be sloppy and inaccurate. Therefore, it is better to cut a nock slightly narrower than needed, and to fine tune using sandpaper. In addition to a sloppy release, a wide nock is likely to have narrow walls that tend to be broken by the string. Second, this technique uses shafts gleaned from boards, so make sure that the nock is at 90° to the annual rings, since then you are less likely to split the shaft with the bowstring.

For the draw weight of the bows that we are making, a simple wrapping of cotton or strong thread below the base of the arrow nock is all that is needed to reinforce it. With heavyweight bows, often slivers of horn are incorporated into the end of the arrow shaft to strengthen it.

Self-Arrows

The arrows described here will be fine with shafts around the smaller diameters. Considering 11/32 in is 8.73mm, shafts in and around this size are a good starting point. It is worth drilling a few holes of perhaps 6mm, 7mm, 8mm and 9mm in a stiff board or metal plate to act as a template to pass your shafts through and achieve consistency – metal washers can help too. (These metric measurements are not commercially available arrow diameters but will get you close, and it is easier to find metric drill bits these days.)

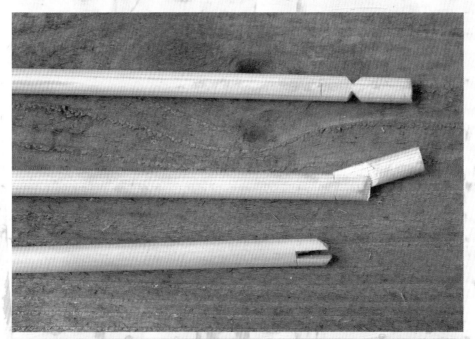

Nocking an arrow.

A variety of woods in various states of readiness.

Some materials can be very stiff relative to their diameter, while some are quite weak and may have to be thicker to stop them wobbling. Hazel is a good example of this: it is easy to find long, straight shafts, but they can be very pithy and weak, and may have to be made quite thick. The very best materials are some of our native shrubs: dogwood, wayfaring tree, guelder rose and wild privet, to name a few. These produce shafts that are very stiff, relative to their diameter.

Arrow Design

There are many profiles of arrow design. You can leave the shafts as found or have them heavier at one end than the other. Normally, the heavy end goes where the point is. This may depend on the type of points that you use: if you're using something fairly lightweight, it may be worth leaving the taper on the shaft; however, if a metal pile is glued on to the already heavy end of a shaft, it may be difficult to make an arrow balanced.

Personally, I prefer to make arrows with an even diameter throughout their length, and I harvest slightly oversized shafts to work down. To me, another advantage of using shrubby species is that normally they don't have an abrupt taper rate and are easier to prepare.

Natural arrow shafts, debarked and drying.

I harvest arrows in batches and look for the straightest that I can find. It is possible to straighten arrows, even those with big kinks in them, but to be honest it is a complete pain. Not only is it difficult to work out extreme bends, but they have a nasty habit of coming back in again. If you pick very straight shafts to begin with, then much effort and cursing can be saved.

To straighten arrows, it is best to let them dry first – green wood will straighten quickly, but it has the habit of moving again as it dries. If you have patience, it is possible to straighten and dry a shaft at the same time, as it is heat that is used to make the wood pliable. Any heat source, from open fires to paint strippers, can be used. There is a common misconception that steam is required to bend wood, but this isn't true – at least, not in my experience with arrows, and indeed, bows. It is a simple process to hold the shaft over a heat source at the point that it needs working and then, using both knees, or whatever is needed, straighten out the kink by manipulation either side. It is important not to heat to the point of scorching at this stage or the shaft might break.

Selecting and Preparing the Shafts
Look for shafts close to the finished diameter to save work paring them down, but not so close that shrinkage from drying will make them too small. All shafts will lose some girth as they dry, but with bigger ones this seems to be more noticeable. Check each shaft as you harvest and avoid those with excessive pith relative to their finished diameter – either that or live with having thicker arrows.

189

Try also, where possible, to avoid shafts with nodes. These are the points where the leaves and branches come out, and they are always a little fiddly. Certainly, large knots should be rejected completely: they make reduction and straightening more hassle than it needs to be. Allow several inches above your finished arrow length just in case you mess up your nock carving.

I remove the bark as soon as the shafts are harvested. I can see no advantage to leaving it on, since for most species bark is harder to remove when it dries. I do understand the argument for leaving the bark on as a means of slowing down drying to prevent splitting, but personally have never found splitting to be a big problem.

Rolling the Arrow

When ready, the shafts can be reduced to a linear diameter throughout their length. I find that removal of large amounts of wood is best achieved by rolling the arrow under a decent craft knife. With even pressure, the resulting groove can be cut to a regular depth throughout. Scraping or sanding down past this tool mark helps maintain a circular and even cross-section. Otherwise, a scraper and sandpaper may be all that are needed to get the arrow to pass through a hole of the desired size. Try experimenting with hand-spining the arrows, as discussed, or just try your luck and see what happens. Straighten as needed and the arrows are ready for nocking, in preparation for accepting the string.

It is worth reiterating that matching arrows for a batch that is to be shot from the same bow is simpler using the same species from the same location. However, in theory, if your spining and weighing are correct, then any arrows from any source should be perfectly fine when shot from your bow.

Nocking the arrows also can be done in the same way as described above, although there is no need to worry about the string splitting the shaft with bad orientation of the nock. You may wish to use natural fibres to reinforce the base of the nock.

Fletching

The basic purpose of the feathers on an arrow is to cause drag, ensuring the back of the arrow follows the front. The longer the shot, the more apparent the effect of fletching. At very short distances, it is possible to be accurate without fletching.

lling the arrow under a craft knife.

The size and shape of your fletching will vary, depending on the sort of archery in which you are interested. If flight shooting (seeing how far you can shoot) is your thing, then minimal fletching would be your choice. If you are looking for accuracy over shorter distances, then longer, higher fletching is key.

In a nutshell, the bigger the fletching, the more drag, and therefore the more stability and accuracy. The trade-off is that the extra drag means the arrow won't go so far or so fast, and the extra size means that it is more affected by wind and rain.

I tend not to shoot for distance, largely because I can't be bothered to go and fetch the arrows. The following assumes that you are using 5–6in (12.7–15.2cm) fletching, which is a good, versatile size in my opinion. When an arrow leaves the bow, it spins in the air just as a rifle bullet does, with this rifling motion helping to keep the arrow on target. Some archers prefer spiral fletching, which exaggerates this spin. Such fletching is fiddlier to fit and causes even more drag than conventional fletching. However, the principle is sound, and helps to underline the need to have fletching that allows this spin to happen.

All fletching on the same arrow must come from the same wing of the bird selected. Picture a bird's wing. It curves over towards the tips and orientates the feather in that plane. As with most things, it is possible to buy feathers online – some of them specifically for archery. These range from finished and dyed feathers that are ready to go, to much larger and more complete feathers for making hats and decorations.

Using a Fletching Jig

If you intend to carry on in archery and make lots of arrows, it is worth investing in a fletching jig. This allows accurate placement of each feather. Three are generally used, at precisely 120° apart. The first feather placed on the arrow shaft is known as the 'cock feather'. This is set at 90° to the arrow knock, assuming – as is often the case in traditional archery – that the hand holding the bow is also the arrow rest. When shooting, the cock feather is placed on the hand facing out from the bow. This is to minimise the chance of the fletching slapping the bow and being deflected on release.

...e cock feather.

When using a fletching jig, the arrow shaft can be set so that the first fletching to be fixed is the cock feather. Many archers make this feather a different colour, so it's very easy to place when shooting, although this is not strictly necessary. Many glues are available specifically for fletching, but I find ordinary superglue is just as effective. Using the jig allows simple rotation for the remaining two feathers to be placed accurately. A wrap of cotton over the base of the fletching to reduce their potential to cut your 'arrow rest', and the process is complete.

All that remains is to cut the arrow to length, and then fit the point. Aim for a length of arrow that, when drawn back, leaves an inch or so beyond the bow. This is to avoid drawing the arrow, releasing and shooting yourself in the hand at point-blank range – definitely an eye-watering experience! I find that if I make my arrows 29in (72.5cm) long, I can shoot them quite comfortably. Some people keep their arrows longer than this, but I find that this makes them much harder to spine correctly. There is

Using the jig.

A finished fletching.

always the chance of overdrawing too, and breaking the bow, especially if you let anyone else shoot it. I also oil the shafts of my arrows to prevent them taking in water.

The process is largely the same with a primitive arrow, which indeed can be fletched using a jig or tied on, as explained below.

Natural Feathers
For archery, the big primary feathers are the ones to choose, as they are usually the stiffest. They are also responsible for powered flight, and this need to push air means that they are very densely locked near to the shaft.

These feathers are found beyond the last joint of the wing and are asymmetrical. For arrows, as mentioned previously, the feathers need to be from the same wing. The bigger the bird, the bigger the primaries, and the more options are available. The feathers of birds that live on or near water are also highly prized, since they have a highly developed waterproofing system that involves coating their plumage with oil from a preen gland. This oil adds to the dense mat closest to the shaft, which can be seen if the feather is held up to the light. Oil has the effect of making the feather robust in the face of wind and rain; as a fletching, it is less likely to lay flat to the arrow shaft in bad weather.

In my experience, the best birds for fletching feathers are the big waterbirds, such as large ducks and geese. I have had success with gull feathers too, but at a pinch any larger bird will work. It is possible to find feathers in the countryside and on kill sites, and with a little practice it is easy to recognise left- and right-wing primaries. Turkey feathers are widely available online for archery, but at Christmas time approaching a farmer might gain good results.

The use of natural feathers requires some preparation before they can be attached to the arrow shaft.

- First, the feather needs to be split and shaped. This can be done by starting the split with a sharp knife and splitting the quill in a way very similar to preparing roots (as explained in Chapter 5).

- If the quill is old and dry, this may be a real struggle, in which case the entire quill can be cut with a fine-bladed knife or scalpel.

- Whichever method is chosen, the flat side of the quill will have to be reduced further to fit the arrow shaft. This is best done with sandpaper. (For the purist, a smooth sandstone rock can do the same job.)

- Now, the feather can be trimmed to size. Depending on your ability, this is achieved with anything from a craft knife and a straight edge (often the neatest option), to a flint flake used freehand.

Splitting the feather.

There are many weird and funky feather shapes, but I suggest a simple shield design, looking like a triangle, 6in (15cm) long and perhaps 1in (25mm) high. This shape is much easier to cut accurately than most others on offer and looks quite traditional. Depending on how the fletching is to be fixed, a small sliver of featherless quill can be left on either end, to bind the fletching to the shaft. The more uniform and similar in size and shape the feathers are, the better the arrow will perform. It might be wise to use a template to cut the feathers to shape and size.

You can attach the feather in a variety of ways, from merely binding each end, binding each end and across the vanes, using glue and binding, to using superior modern glues that can hold the fletching with no assistance. All of these can be used in conjunction with a modern jig, as previously discussed. To be perfectly honest, I would treat both self-arrows and natural fletching as described above. It is possible to attach the feathers without a jig, but I advise at least the use of a bulldog clip or similar for consistency.

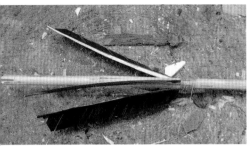

ɔound feather with no glue.

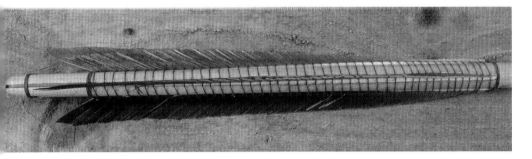

ɔound and glued arrow.

Numbers of fletchings may vary slightly, but the traditional three is probably the easiest and most effective. With this method, start with the cock feather set at 90° to the nock. It is important to leave room for fingers between the end of the arrow shaft and the feathers; it is also important to make sure that the fletching all faces the same way. I have seen both errors on the courses I teach, and more than once.

Without modern glues, binding the feathers is the best option. Glues made from natural materials are often water soluble, weak or extremely messy to apply in delicate operations – it is quite possible to return from an arrow-making session tarred and feathered!

Once the feathers are secured, the bindings can be liberally coated with an adhesive of choice. Again, this could be superglue or pitch, depending on taste and the arrow being made. Bindings may consist of cotton, silk, sinew, false sinew, or finely prepared plant or tree fibres.

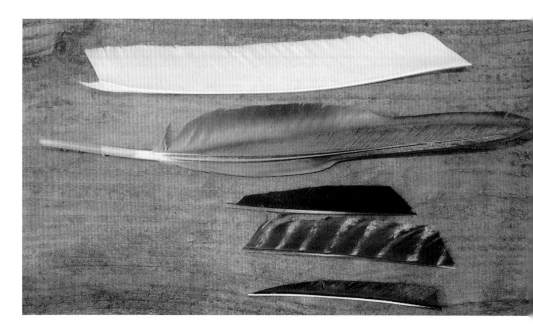

From the top: a bought, extra-long fletching; a Canada goose primary feather; a shield fletching, made from a goose feather; fletching made from a bought feather; a bought fletching, trimmed and ready to go.

Points

I have not concerned myself with Stone Age points here. It is not my intention to recreate the past, just to help in the construction of a bow and arrow that can be shot. Flint and bone points take a lot of time to make, and often break if they hit anything other than a target. If they do hit the target, they are also apt to destroy it.

I mostly roam around the woods shooting at stumps and other landscape features, so I need arrows that allow me to do this time and again. However, if you would like an authentic Stone Age arrow, bone and antler points can be made with relatively little skill using hacksaws and files to abrade the shapes. Be aware that using a metal knife on bone or antler will blunt the knife very quickly.

Modern alternatives exist in the form of target piles. These are great, as they are designed not to stick too deeply into the target so that they can be easily removed. For most purposes, I use taper-fit brass bullet points weighing 100 grains. These require the shaping of the end of the arrow into a cone, which can be done by carving or using a taper tool – basically, a very expensive pencil sharpener.

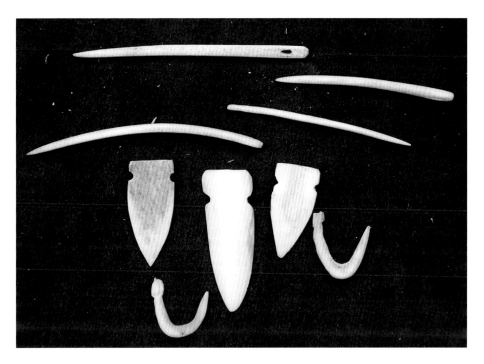

Many implements, including arrowheads and spear points, can be made from bone and antler.

There are many arrow points available to the modern archer.

Depending on the style of archery, blunts can be made from brass caps and other bits and bobs you may find lying around. I tend to secure the point I use with Gorilla Glue, as I have lost the least number of arrowheads since I started using it; pretty much all the other glues I have used would leave heads stuck in the targets. It is worth considering drilling and using a small tack as a back-up when you are fixing the piles.

Whatever point you choose; its weight must be consistent for a consistent spine and arrow flight. The good thing about manufactured points is that this can be relied on.

5

Bark, Roots and Withies

Once upon a time, there was no internet, hard though that is to imagine now. If you were keen to learn new things, you had to rely on word-of-mouth recommendations, scour second hand bookshops for obscure titles, and locate book dealers who were prepared to keep an eye out for works of interest.

It was during this period that I became interested in working with bark, but very little was being done with the material in the UK. When the subject did come up in bushcraft circles – bear in mind that those circles were tiny, in fact, they were more like 'a' circle – it was usually birch bark that people had experienced.

By now, I was frustrated on two fronts. First, I lacked suitable material, as finding enough birch bark of the right quality in the UK was very difficult. Second, I had no idea how to produce some of the things I had seen made from the stuff. At the time, I was working with someone who knew a couple of weaves, but he wouldn't show me. However, I managed to acquire, and then retro-engineer, a woven knife sheath, which taught me that pattern. I also read in an excellent green woodwork book by Mike Abbot about using the inner bark of an elm as chair seating.

This was a real eureka moment for me. As a working woodsman, I knew lots of barks that came off in sheets, and I figured I could make weaving strips from these. The key difference was that the inner bark (or phloem) was being described as the material of choice. Once I had this material and understood its properties, I was away. No more clandestine acquisition of second-hand woven products for me!

I found that many traditional weaves for flat materials, such as those designed around rushes, worked perfectly for bark strips too. A reference in another green woodwork book, this time by Drew Langsner, set me on the road to folded containers.

Bark projects.

Bark

Preparation

Despite my previous comments, it is possible to use some outer barks from the UK, but it remains quite difficult to find material that is thick enough. Birch and cherry would be the two main possibilities but do bear in mind that cherry has huge lenticels, and these become holes in the bark when it is removed from the tree. This makes the material liable to tear and limits its use, especially when folded across one of those weak spots.

For these reasons, the work described below uses inner bark. This is the area just between the coarse dead-looking outer bark and the wood itself. The role of this material is the transportation of sugars around the tree. It is a very thin layer, relative to the overall diameter of the tree, but once it is removed from the circumference of the tree, the tree dies. This process is often called 'ring barking'. Removal of this layer can be caused by hungry deer, squirrels or rabbits eating the bark, or deer rubbing their antlers and forehead scent glands on it. It also can happen in spring, when the bark is at its loosest and weary campers tie their hammocks to thin-barked trees with thin cords, rubbing the bark away during their relaxing nocturnal musings.

All trees have this layer, but in some species, it is possible to remove the inner bark in large sheets. Due to its function, removing quantities of inner bark causes considerable damage to the tree, so it is best to take it only from trees that have been, or will be, felled. It also follows that if you mess up your felling direction when bringing down a tree and slide one tree down another, it puts that neighbouring tree in severe danger due to bark loss.

Similarly, I do not recommend taking just part of the bark from a section of trees, as it still opens the trees up to all kinds of problems. Indeed, I think this is also true of removing outer bark, even though in theory doing so would not kill the tree. However, it takes a good deal of skill not to mess up the process (and, in any case, leaving the tree looking awful will only encourage machete-wielding lunatics to 'have at' the forest with increased vigour).

Spring and early summer are the best times for taking bark since, as mentioned previously, this is when it is at its loosest due to 'rising sap'. What is more important is knowing how to check if your tree is ready to be peeled. If you are in any doubt, cut a small wand or branch, and see if the bark comes away easily. If it is properly loose, often you can do this just with your fingernails.

Taking the bark off before felling.

Bear in mind that bark mirrors the wood beneath it. If you have a twisted and knotty piece of wood, you will have twisted and knotty bark, which will be difficult to work. Also be aware that the larger the diameter of your timber, the thicker its bark – to the point where it may become unusable for craftwork, as it can be too thick to bend or go round corners. However, sometimes you'll find that the bark at the top of the tree is suitable for one project, and the material at the base for another.

Selecting Bark

So, now it's time to choose your wood. Select as straight a pole as possible. It needs to have a diameter of up to 10in (25cm) for the folded projects described below, but 4in (10cm) is usually fine for weaving, and around ½ –2in (12–50mm) straight from the tree works for cordage. These sizes are rough guides. You'll find the amount of recoverable bark is very variable: for example, I have just cut a small pole of around 4in (10cm) diameter to make something specifically for this book, and the bark on it was exceptionally thick.

Sometimes it is worth taking bark off before the tree is felled, since some bark will be damaged or even destroyed by the felling process; however, this is only beneficial if you are making folded containers and considering leaving on the outer bark. For weaving projects, the bark should be left on the tree, and only removed after the pole is felled and the outer bark is removed. It is much easier to remove material from a log, which will give you something to push against.

There are many species that can be used to collect bark, but some, such as oak, are slow-growing and have very thick outer bark, which can be difficult to remove. Oaks are also valuable timber trees, so be aware that foresters don't take kindly to turning tomorrow's quality furniture into today's baskets. I list here a few trees that produce good material, but the beauty of this subject is the opportunity that it provides for experimentation, so do try out other species too:

- birch
- cherry
- Lawson's cypress
- lime
- sweet chestnut

- sycamore
- western red cedar
- willow
- wych elm.

The inner bark of all of these trees also produces cordage and, when their wood is dry, tinder, both of which are discussed later in this chapter.

Removing the Bark
For weaving projects, the outer bark must be removed: your material will be far too stiff to be workable if you leave it on. For folded projects, the outer bark can be left on for all the species mentioned above, although when I do so with bark from all but the conifers, I find it difficult to keep a decent shape to my containers when the material dries. The rim of folded containers made from broadleaf trees with the outer bark removed always seems to pucker.

To remove the outer bark, you need a relatively blunt instrument. I have experimented a lot over the years and have concluded that the back of a closed, folding-saw blade is as good a tool as any other. Try out different angles. The trick is to remove the outer bark without damaging the phloem layer (inner bark) directly underneath, since the latter is our raw material. Sometimes, trying not to be too heavy-handed can be a challenge, especially if you are feeling all pumped up and gladiatorial, having felled the tree on which you're working.

Once you have removed all the outer bark, use a knife to slit the inner bark the full length of the pole: make sure you cut right down to the wood. If you have a feature such as a knot in the wood, you should make this the focus of the split, to make maximum use of sound material – it effectively puts the knot on the edge of the sheet. You may or may not have stripped the outer layer to the pole's full extent – in which case, make sure that you cut the circumference down to the timber. If any is left attached, it is quite likely to tear the bark as it is removed. With thick bark or material with the outer layer left on, it may be easier to use a saw to achieve this.

Now it should be fairly straightforward to ease off this material. I normally reverse the knife to lift the bark either side of the split, then finish easing it off gently with my fingers. You may find that making a spud (a piece of wood shaped like a screwdriver) is useful here. If the material is

1. Use a blunt instrument to remove the outer layer.
2. Slit lengthways using a knife and then use a spud to ease the bark off.
3. Once you have started to remove the bark, it is often easier to use your hands.

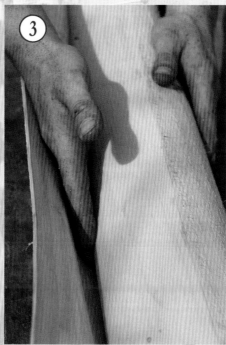

too tightly fixed, it may be possible to pound it gently or pour hot water over it as a means of loosening things up a bit. (Personally, I think it is just easier to wait until the season advances a bit further and the bark loosens of its own accord.)

At this point, you should have a rectangular piece of inner bark that resembles wet leather in look and feel. It is a remarkable material, quite unlike anything else.

Weaving the Bark

To begin weaving, you will need to cut the material into strips of even width. Bear in mind that the more uniform these strips are, the tighter and neater the weave will be. Indeed, it is impossible to make anything properly tightly woven unless the strips are even. You can use a straight edge to ensure regularity or experiment, as I have done, with a leather strip cutter.

To achieve the same end in a slightly more rustic fashion, you could make a little gauge that works in conjunction with your knife. These are

driven into the annual rings of a stump and the knife driven in beside this. The distance between the gauge and the knife is the thickness of the strips produced. If you are very skilled with tools, you may even be able to do this freehand.

For weaving, the narrower your strips, the tighter and neater the weave will be. However, there also will be lots more ends to deal with, which may be confusing until you get your head around the pattern. Around ¼–½in (6–12mm) width is a good compromise and starting point. Start with as long a piece of bark as possible since this allows you to make taller containers. You could add in new material as you go along, but it never looks very neat.

A simple, carved thickness gauge, which can be driven into a log and used with a knife.

straight edge or a leather cutter can be used.

At this point, your material will be wonderfully pliant, but it soon turns back into wood, so you'll have to work fairly quickly. Unfortunately, if it is woven too wet, it will shrink, and the weave will open up. There is a balance to meet here, which is best achieved through experimenta-tion. Happily, at any point, the material can be re-wetted and will become pliant again. Bear in mind that if this is overdone, then the material rapidly becomes too wet and will shrink excessively again: normally, a quick dunk in warm water or running damp hands over it is sufficient.

The conifers, especially Western red cedar, will stay more pliant when dry, and arguably make the best weaving materials. It is possible to split the strips in half, as shown below, if they are too thick to bend easily. Use the same technique as for splitting wood; lean on the fat side more to cor-rect any splits running out to the side of the material.

Clockwise from top left: Splitting bark; Willow can be dyed using its own outer bark (see Chapter 7); Bark ready for working.

Weaving Projects

I have outlined several projects to get you started on weaving. In the following, I show you how to make a quiver for arrows or sheath for your knife, a flat-bottomed container, which, unlike the quiver, is free standing and finally, some folded containers. However, before starting on any of these, get a feel for your materials by learning how to make this simple strap.

Project 1: Strap
Bark strips can be used to make belts and straps, and it's a very simple process. It is easiest to hold the strips in a split stick for plaiting.

- Start with the outer weaver, bringing it sharply over at a 45° angle to get the tightest and flattest finish.

- Take the second weaver and repeat the process, then the third, and so on.

- Once you are down to the final weaver, use it to start the process going back the other way.

- To finish the project, weave the ends back in on themselves.

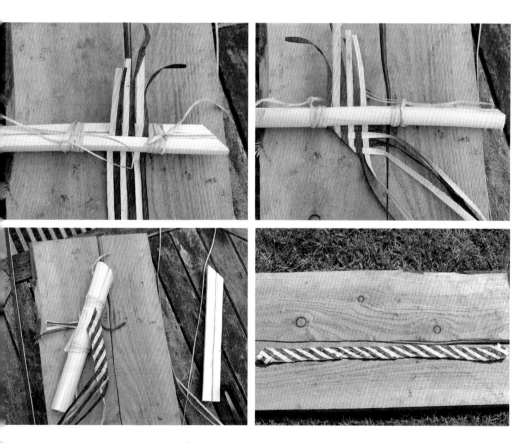

Use a stick to hold the strips of bark.   2. Start at one edge and weave across, until only one strip remains. Use that last strip to change direction and keep repeating this process.   4. Weave the ends back in to finish off ur strap.

Alternatively, you can weave the ends into other objects – to serve as carrying straps, for example, for the projects below. This can work well, but the strap and basket strips must be the same width, otherwise, you'll find it hard to make them look neat or, more importantly, to hold.

In these images I have used willow bark, some of which is dyed and some undyed, to create an attractive contrast.

Project 2: Quiver or Knife Sheath
To make a quiver or knife sheath, do the following:

1. Start by taking several strips and folding them in half. The longer the strips, the better, as it means that there will be less need to add in material later.

2. Cross one strip through another at the point of folding.

3. Continue to add strips in a chequerboard pattern. In essence, the number of strips added gives you the width of your container.

4. Keep turning the work over to ensure the chequerboard pattern is the same on both sides.

Once you have the desired width, it is time to start weaving the container proper: we are now going up, to create height, rather than increasing width by going outwards:

5. Lay the work flat.

6. Starting at the last weaver you added in, peel back the top individual strand to reveal its partner underneath. It is this partner that gets bent over at a 45° angle, to be woven under and over through the other weavers.

7. Once this has been done, turn the whole thing over and work the original weaver, the one that was pulled out of the way, into the weave. You must always finish with pairs, as this locks the weave into place.

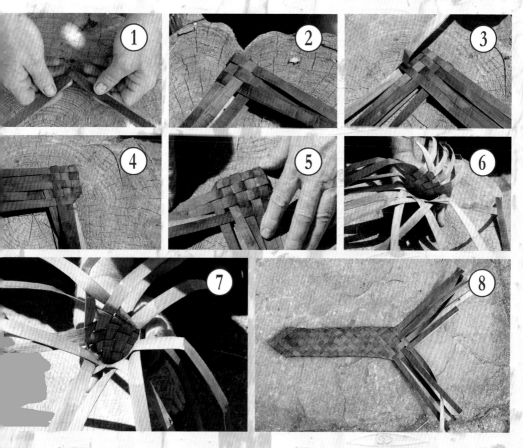

Fold strips in half and cross them over each other.

Continue adding strips in a chequerboard pattern.

Peel back the top weaver of a pair.

Weave the strip from below it through the other weavers.

Turn your workpiece over and weave the top strip to join its partner.

Repeat this on the other corner and a pocket should be formed.

Continue the process. To finish, weave back down the container as described for the next project.

An almost finished quiver.

8. Next, go to the opposite side of the quiver and repeat the process.

9 Once both sides have been done, you should have created a pocket. The first locking weave is then simply repeated until the desired height is achieved, or the material runs out.

Always work the edge weavers and always make certain you finish with pairs to ensure success. This is quite a complex process to explain, so just work through the description in conjunction with the previous images.

Project 3: Flat-Bottomed Woven Container
This project is slightly more elaborate than the quiver: the finished container is a free-standing basket. The key to making it is that, although laid out in a square, it is the corners that go up to start the weave, with each corner interlocking with the next. (It is possible to make rectangular baskets when you are more experienced.)

1. Start with an even number of strips, and in relatively small numbers, so that you can keep track of things: having thirty or forty ends to worry about can be taxing.

2. Tie everything together into a square, so you can see where the corners are.

3. Firmly crease the bends into the material when bringing up the sides. Once the corners 'go up', it is relatively easy to rotate the basket in your hands and weave over and under, under and over.

4. Finish by folding the ends and weaving them back on themselves. (This is the same for the quiver and can be done on the inside of your basket, if there is room.)

The downside of working with inner bark is that there is always a smoother side, where the bark was close to the tree, and a rougher side, where the outer layer has been scraped away. Where this shows in the finished item may be a consideration when you are deciding which way to turn in the ends.

1. Tie off the weave into an even square.
2. Fold up two of the corners.
3–4. Weave these corners into each other.
5–6. Bring the other two corners up and weave these in also.
7. Continue until the desired height is reached, and then weave back to finish.
8. Finished containers.

Project 4: Folded Containers

In many ways, folded containers are simpler and quicker to make than woven ones, but there are a couple of secrets to success. First, never score the bark in the same plane as it runs up and down the tree, only fold it. Just as wood is easier to split than to crosscut, so is bark. Even the lightest pencil mark can cause bark to tear or break off completely, if worked from top to bottom. Second, don't try to stitch the container together until it has dried a little. Movement during drying can cause tight stitches to split the basket; in a similar vein, and for a similar reason, it is a bad idea to line up the stitch holes on the longitudinal plane. At the very least, be sure to space them well.

Two folded designs are described here. One is a flat-bottomed folded container that will stand upright on its own; the other is a berry-gathering basket whose bottom is designed to fit over your thigh when held in place by a neck strap. The idea, I guess, was to keep the hands free. This basket can be made narrower and will work perfectly well as a quiver.

Berry Basket

1. Start with a perfect rectangle of bark.

2. Find the centre point of the rectangle and mark a line through it. This must be very lightly done to avoid the container folding at this point. This is the reference point from which the base is marked out. (Usually, to mark out the base, I use a suitably sized bowl or plate. The idea is to mark out an oval since a circle is actually very difficult to fold around without tearing the bark.)

3. It should be apparent from the images below that 1in (25mm) or so is left over at the ends of the oval where a V-cut is made. This 'V' folds in on itself, allowing the sides to overlap; later they will be stitched together.

4. Score the oval on the opposite side to the direction of the fold. Again, I recommend that this be done gently.

5. If, when the sides are bent up, the oval shape doesn't appear as a line on the inside of the container, then score a little deeper. It is better to have a couple of attempts at scoring, rather than to cut so deep that the whole thing falls apart.

6. Coax the sides gently up and have the oval base 'pop' into the concavity where your thigh will sit. It may be that both hands bring up the side while the knee is used to push up the base. (Done right, the craftsman looks every bit as cool as the Karate Kid.)

7. Once the sides are up, overlap them, peg the top, tie the sides and allow to dry a little.

1. Help yourself with the marking out by using a suitable plate. Don't forget the 'V' cuts.
2. Gently ease the side up to pop the base.
3. You should be left with a concave base.
4. Peg, tie and dry your basket.

The longer the piece of bark you use for this project, the taller the finished basket will be. The larger the girth of the tree, the wider your basket. Bear in mind that the quest for bigger trees and wider containers might be at the cost of thick bark that is too hard to fold.

Flat-Bottomed Container

Many of the same rules that govern making the berry basket also apply to the flat-bottomed container. Be sure to start with a good rectangle and score only across, not along, the grain. The other key point is that the sides of the container must overlap each other. If we assume, for the sake of easy maths, that the base of the container is square, this means each side (the bit that looks like a bat wing) must be at least 1in (25mm) longer than half of the length (or width) of the base. I haven't given measurements in these descriptions as I think it is easier, and indeed less frustrating, to adapt the size to fit whatever bark you have managed to collect.

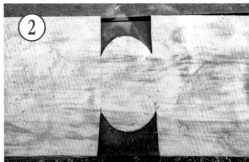

1. Mark out a square with two semicircles that will form the side flaps.
2. Cut out the shape, leaving wings that reach at least half again the length of the sides.
3. Gently fold, tie and leave to dry.

Once the sides are up, they can be pegged, tied or both, and should be left to dry a little. If your container is to be left for a significant time, it is worth pegging in some fairly thick bark strips to ensure that the rim stays circular, otherwise it is very likely to become corrugated. This can be done with clothes pegs or partially split sticks.

The stitch holes themselves can be made with anything from a sharpened stick to a cordless drill. A knife will tend to go through suddenly and may tear the bark too much. Personally, I prefer a palm drill or an awl with a slight drill point, since they give the best control. Stitching is greatly aided by using a very large needle if you can find one.

Stitching Folded Projects

Thin bark strips, cordage and roots can all be used for stitching, depending how Stone Age you want to be. Experiment with patterns, but I like to use a long lace, doubled and stitched in an 'X' pattern, such that one end of the doubled lace crosses the other inside the container.

Palm drills, awls and needles.

1. Start at the bottom and tighten as you go.
2. Leave a big gap between stitches to avoid splitting the bark.

Different stitched finishes: A bark rim finishes off your basket nicely.

On a narrow-necked or exceptionally tall container, it may be necessary to put the stitching in loose at the base of the container, then tighten up as more stitches are added, as it may not be possible to reach to the bottom if it is tightly closed up.

The same rule applies to stitching on a bark rim, for which it is worth marking out the stitch holes first to get them equally spaced. (Incidentally, I have experimented with wooden hoops for rims, but I can never make them as neat as bark.) With some thicker barks, especially conifers, the rim may not be needed, but it does finish the baskets off nicely. Normally, separate laces will be needed for the rim and the sides, and for the flat-bottomed container I also stitch the flaps on separately.

Cordage

Having gone this far into the joys of bark, doubtless you'll have thought to yourself, 'I bet you could tie stuff up with this'. You'd be right. Stripped straight off the tree or branch, with no other preparation, not even

removal of the outer layer, bark can be used as a rough binding. In fact, I have used it to make sweat lodge frames that stayed together for several seasons. The strap explained earlier in the chapter, and variants of it, can also be extended to produce very strong ties.

Traditionally, the finest cordage is made from the inner bark. This can be obtained exactly as described above. It is important to go for very thin wands – perhaps as thick as your thumb – and to be very gentle, so as not to destroy the thin inner layer while removing the outer layer. The layer needs to be thin because otherwise the strips you cut for making into cordage will become very difficult to roll into a cylinder during the making process.

Retting also occurs naturally.

Lime and cedar retted and ready for use as cordage or tinder.

The other traditional method for obtaining bark for cordage is to ret or partially rot the material in water, either in a stream or a barrel. This can take several weeks and can be very smelly, but the results are quite incredible as the bark delaminates, becoming paper thin and very workable. Arguably, it makes superior cordage, as the fineness of the strands creates lots of fibre-to-fibre friction and intertwining, leading to a stronger finished product.

Many trees can be retted, but perhaps the best – and certainly the best known – is lime, which delaminates into incredibly thin layers that are twisted easily (as described below). It is even possible to find naturally retted cordage hanging from dead limes and other branches, all ready to go.

Making Cordage

To make cordage, ensure that the fibres you start with are a uniform thickness throughout. It is also important that, when twisting, everything travels in the same direction – sudden changes of direction mean that a cord is easily unwound. Many people suggest that if you begin twisting at exactly the halfway point, you will create a weak point. I disagree. Friction throughout the whole length of the cord is the thing that holds it together. That said, it is much easier to add fibres by staggering joints.

In the following, I describe the sequence of making cordage as I would do it, as a right-handed person who always twists towards himself. Bear this in mind if you want to adapt the process to your own particular style.

- Select a uniform bundle of fibres. Slightly past the halfway point, clamp them tightly in your left hand.

- Twist the bundles towards you using your right hand, until the action of pushing your right hand towards your left causes the fibre to kink. This is the start of the two-strand cordage. By pushing your hands together, the cord should start to wrap around itself. If you hold the point where this starts, you can help the twist to get maximum tension.

- Now you should have an inch or so of two-strand cordage. Using the thumb and forefinger of your left hand, grasp the point at which the cordage finishes, and the two strands start.

- Taking one strand in your right hand, twist again, keeping the cordage that has already been made in your left hand from moving.

- Once you have tension on the strand, slot it between the third and fourth fingers of your left hand: it is very important that you do not allow this twist to unwind.

- At this point, you should have a small amount of cordage clamped firmly in your left hand between the thumb and forefinger, along with one strand under tension and clamped between your third and fourth fingers.

1. Twist your material until the fibres kink.
2. Help the process along.
3. Grasp firmly at the point where the cordage ends and twist one strand.
4. Twist the second strand, so that both strands are under tension.
5. Hold the two strands tight and release the cordage, encouraging it to twist.

Opposite: Adding in.

- Now, pick up the remaining untwisted strand with your right hand, then twist and put tension on it. The tricky part is to grab the first strand while still clutching the second, then let go with your left hand. This should create a counter-twist that wraps the fibres into cordage. Once again, this can be helped along to ensure maximum tension.

- Repeat the process until one of the strands starts to run out: more fibres then need to be added in.

Adding In

To add in is a relatively simple process. Simply lay one new fibre across the tail end of the strand that is running out and twist them both in together. It is worth tapering the ends when adding in to avoid creating an ugly bulge. Adding in is important not only when fibres run out, but also if one strand becomes much thinner than another. If strands are unequal in diameter, the smaller strand merely wraps around the thicker one, producing inferior cordage.

Tinder

Dead, dry inner bark works well as tinder. It can be removed from dead trees and logs by scraping with a knife, or by breaking the outer bark and pulling strips out, or simply collected, depending on how loose the material is and, to some extent, the species of tree. Outer bark can also be great for tinder, especially from shrubby climbers such as honeysuckle and clematis, which can be buffed to a very fine consistency by rubbing it in your hands using a sock-washing motion. (Where I am based, I tend to avoid honeysuckle, as it is used as nest material by dormice, which are a protected species – very cute and they make me feel guilty for stealing their beds.)

The oil-rich (and therefore flammable) outer bark of both birch and cherry is a superb fire-lighting material, although care must be taken not to damage the delicate inner layer when harvesting (as discussed earlier). Thus, it is best only to peel bark that is being shed naturally, especially on a live tree. Even then, with cherry, there is a tendency for the bark to tear into the tree when you try to remove it; for this reason, I tend to cut off the peeling curls of cherry bark.

Roots

Roots have an amazing structure that is incredibly good at resisting forces trying to pull the parent plant out of the ground. Someone worked out, I have no idea how, that a 2in tree root could lift an elephant. My guess is that it could lift a big one, at that.

For craft purposes, roots work like nature's wire and can be used for bindings of all kinds. Very small, thin roots can be twisted into cordage that is very strong and slightly elastic. If enough are gathered, even small baskets can be woven using them.

In my experience, conifer roots are the best for our purposes, as they seem to be the straightest and have the fewest side roots and kinks. The next best come from birch. However, in theory, any root is worth a try. It is fairly obvious that, with roots especially, you should adhere to the basic principle of gathering from as far and wide as possible. What we are after are the feeder roots, because although we are unlikely to fell a tree with overenthusiastic harvesting, we could certainly affect its vigour.

Pull and tear the bark to break open its fibres. 2. Use the sock-washing method to get finer strands.
The longer you work, the finer it all becomes.

Clockwise from above: Peeling bark from a birch tree; You can make tinder
by rolling old birch into a sausage and carving coils off it; If the birch is not
peeling, scraping bark from a dead log still yields results; A bundle of mixed
tinder consisting of honeysuckle and clematis; Scraping with a knife is
great for dead inner bark; Depending on the quality of the bark, breaking out
the outer layer and then buffing may be the best option.

Harvesting roots for woodcraft.

Roots should be debarked using the back of a knife or a 'V'-shaped stick.

With a small digging stick, it is a relatively simple matter to scrape away the surface of the soil and reveal the roots underneath. For the project described below, roots of 1/8–¼in (3–5mm) diameter should be big enough but, as with all weaving, the longer they are, the better, since it saves you trying to add fibres in later. The roots we need are not especially deep but do remember to refill any holes you've made to prevent the root hairs you leave behind drying out.

Roots should be debarked prior to splitting, which is done easily enough with the back of a knife, if you only need one or two. If lots of roots are to be split, shaping a 'V' in a small stick and drawing the roots through it may be faster.

Small roots can be used in the round, but it is better to split bigger roots in two, except when big, chunky projects are the order of the day. Doing so makes both the work easier – and the finished product neater – when you are binding the flat surface of the root to the workpiece.

litting a root.

Project 5: Making a Fish Hook

There are many applications for roots. Here, I have chosen to describe making a fish hook. This is a great little project for becoming familiar with the properties of the materials. Originally, this type of work would have been barbed with a bone point, but I have described how to make a wooden barb.

- Start with a split root and the two elements that make up the fish hook, as shown in the image below.

- The key thing is to point the end of the root towards the corner of the fish hook's shaft. The root goes under the shaft, then comes over it to hold the barb.

Left: Start by carving the barb and the shaft.
1. Point the end of the root to the corner of the hook.
2. Take the root around the base of the shaft.
3. Wrap around to capture the barb.
4. Create a cross and wrap back around the main shaft again.
5. Rotating the piece should 'show' the pattern to create a herringbone.
6. Each rotation repeats the same pattern.
7. Maintain the herringbone throughout the process.
8. Continue until the end of the shaft is covered.
9. Tuck the root back along its own weave to lock off.

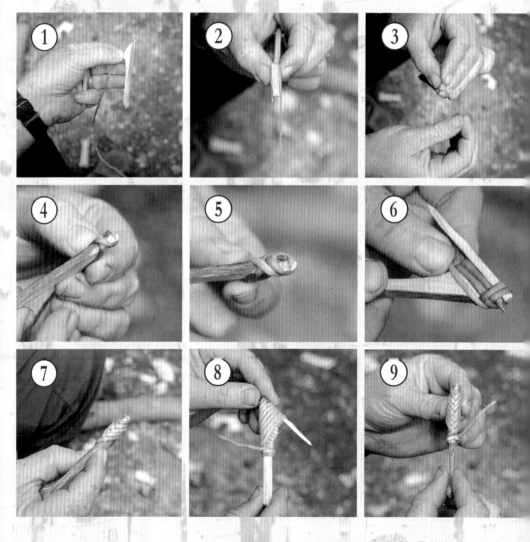

- Once this sequence is established, a little like the flat-bottomed woven container, rotating the work in your hand effectively shows you which path to take.

- Done correctly, there will be a lovely herringbone pattern along the spine of the hook.

Withies

Before string became commonplace in modern times, pretty much everything in the woods would have come out tied and bound using a withy. In a similar way to roots, withies can be used very much like wire, the difference is that they are less flexible. They are made from the small stems of pliant tree species, which are twisted until their fibres have been separated but not severed.

The best species I have tried for this purpose are hazel, birch, willow and rowan. Unless you split it down very finely, it is difficult to tie knots in a withy, but they make great bindings and can be formed into timber hitches and suchlike (for this and other knots, see Chapter 9).

Making them is tough on the hands and forearms, so start with good materials. Check that stems are straight and free of big knots and side branches, since these are likely to break and ruin all your hard work.

I was shown how to make withies by an old Sussex woodsman, who had hands like leathered shovels and forearms like Popeye. Despite his age, he twisted hazel wands like grass as I huffed and puffed, got cramp and left lots of skin on the trees. I did manage to grasp the concept in the end but realise, through my work as a teacher, that for most people this traditional method is all going to be a bit much.

The technique I was shown involves leaving the wand attached to the tree and pulling it to put tension on the wood lengthways. Without this tension, the pressure becomes localised, which usually snaps the withy. Once the tension is applied, the wand is twisted until the fibres are separated but not severed. Often, this can be heard as a crack, and is certainly felt. The next step is to move the arms in a bicycle motion, severing the fibres all the way to the attachment point on the main tree. You then cut the finished withy free. It is the bicycling motion that burns the forearms and shreds the palms.

1. Leaving a needle, twist the stem to separate the fibres.
2. Kink the needle over and use it as a handle.
3. Take this process as far down the wood as possible.
4. Rotate the needle to extend the area of separated fibres.
5. Use the needle to wind the fibres up.
6. Withies can be split when you need to use finer bindings.

My alternative method starts the same way. The wand must be attached to the tree (it would take extraordinary strength to make a withy from a cut stick, even if it were possible at all). The stick is still twisted until the fibres are separated but not severed. But the twist is started slightly lower down, leaving a stiff section above your initial starting point. This serves as a useful needle for the later tying of hitches and lashings, but can also be used as a winding handle, effectively allowing the point at which the fibres are severed to be wound evenly down the stem.

This even twisting is vital to avoid stiff spots that will probably break the withy – or at least make using it as a lashing awkward. Care needs to be taken with this method not to let go, as the withy may unwind suddenly and violently in the vicinity of your face. Whichever method you use, you must keep tension on the stem as you wind it.

The size of the stem selected is very much down to the maker's strength. Larger withies can be split down, so I generally try to make a reasonably thick one to get the pain over with in one go, then split it down to use around camp. In this split-down state, they can be used for basketry, although often the finish will be fairly rough. However, as a biodegradable, extremely strong binding, withies take a lot of beating.

A withy being used as timber hitch.

6

Fire

One of my first experiences of teaching fire to students became one of my most memorable. I was relatively new to the nuances of some of the subject areas, fire by friction being one of them. At a deep psychological level, I feel that this technique won't work unless the practitioner really believes it will. No amount of practice and success in the privacy of your own home can prepare a person for the ring of expectant faces of eager students, waiting to be amazed.

Clearly, on this occasion it all became too much: the anticipation, the build-up, that little voice telling me it couldn't possibly work. And – lo and behold! – it didn't. At least not for the first eleven goes.

Refusing to quit, I just kept going, no doubt boring my audience immensely. Luckily, the twelfth attempt yielded results: a small glowing pile of hot dust. Leaning over and gently wafting air across it to make it grow, a bead of sweat from the previous exertion rolled off my nose on to the powder – and neatly extinguished it.

Feather sticks.

Bow Drill and Hand Drill

Friction is the iconic method of fire-making and one that many students of bushcraft use as a milestone – maybe millstone – in their skill development. It can seem like a lot of hard, sweaty work, and neither the most practical nor the easiest way of getting yourself a fry-up.

On some levels, of course, I agree with this sentiment, but there is also something else to it: the romance of liberating the fire from the forest, the sense of self-reliance, and the bringing together of tree knowledge and tool skills to achieve something. Perhaps I wouldn't embark on a multi-day canoe journey to somewhere notoriously wet and horrible and choose to rely only on this method, but it is still a nice thought that you could do it, if necessary.

The bow drill and hand drill work in a very similar fashion, but arguably, the former has a mechanical advantage in the form of its bow. While both methods need sound technique to work properly, the hand drill is harder to master, partly because only short, skin-destroying practice sessions are possible – assuming the student wants to be able to use their hands to pick anything up afterwards. However, it is also harder because brute force and ignorance seldom work. (While this is also true of the bow drill, to a large extent, I have seen some very strong individuals succeed using frankly rubbish technique.)

The basic technique for both is rotating a round wood drill into a flat hearth board, wearing the wood away to powder and hopefully generating enough heat through friction to create a glowing coal, much like a cigarette end. This black powder falls through a notch cut in the hearth board, from which it is collected and transferred to tinder.

In my experience, the determinants of success can be divided into three distinct areas: correct wood selection, accurate construction of the kit and components, and sound technique.

Selecting the Wood

It is important to remember that anything to do with making fire is reliant for success on the state of the timber. This is true whether you are rubbing sticks together or burning logs. For the best chance of success, choose standing deadwood whenever possible: that is, trees that have died and remain upright in the same position as when they were alive.

The worst timber available for fires is the stuff lying in direct contact with the ground, which will have been soaking up moisture like a sponge. Along with many other things in life, this rule can be bent slightly to match circumstances. If, for example, it has been a blistering English summer (as we all know, this happens a lot …) with temperatures hot enough to make a scorpion sweat, and if this heat has continued for weeks on end, it is perfectly possible to pick sticks straight up from the ground and burn them. However, without these perfect conditions, even when standing deadwood is wet on the outside, it can be split down to reveal a relatively dry centre from which both firewood and friction sets can be fashioned.

Adjust your gathering to take account of recent weather conditions and type of wood, and anywhere between these two extremes can be made to burn.

Some woods are easier to make fire with than others, and generally, lower density equals higher chance of success. However, if you are not careful, you can end up practising with the easier species, and find yourself stuck there. Choosing medium-density wood will make you work harder, but it also means that you are forced to look at both the component parts and your technique more critically to ensure success. (When it comes to using a hand drill, I would try the easiest combinations available, just because it hurts too much not to!)

The list below ranks tree species from easiest to hardest and assumes a drill and hearth board made of the same wood. Spookily enough, this is a hotly debated topic among the fire-by-friction fraternity: should the drill be made of a harder wood than the hearth, or vice versa? In reality, it doesn't matter, but if you are going to use a different drill wood, try to select one that is harder – or rather, denser – than the board, otherwise your drill will wear down at a rapid rate and become unusable very quickly.

There are pros and cons to both approaches, not least that harder woods take more effort to carve. Mixing densities means that you must find two different species of the right quality to be able to make your set. Conversely, drills take longer to make than boards, so it may make sense to have your drill as the component most resistant to wearing down. In dry weather, it is often possible to find a straight stick of the correct diameter, shape the ends, and then away you go. Obviously, if it has been raining for a long time, this may not be possible.

With a bow drill, using the same drill and hearth woods is usually advantageous, and generally my preferred way of going about things. As the board must be relatively broad, it means finding a large piece of wood. I split such a piece down the middle, getting a board from one half and, by quartering the other half, enough material for two drills. This also means that the easily crushed and worn-down pith at the centre of all trees is pushed over to the side of the drill or even removed completely, making the whole thing much more robust.

Any wood selected should be as dry as possible, and not so hard that an indent cannot be made with the fingernail. Some degree of decay is essential – a fact that is especially noticeable when using harder woods. Timber that is collected green and then dried indoors always seems to be a different prospect to timber that has been found dry in the woods and used.

using a larger piece of wood, the hearth board can be made from one half, and two drills from the other.

The following lists a variety of wood, ranging from easy to hard, and assumes your drill and hearth are to be made of the same wood:

1. lime
2. clematis
3. ivy
4. horse chestnut
5. western red cedar
6. buddleia
7. sycamore
8. alder
9. willow
10. birch
11. spruce
12. rhododendron
13. gorse

14. holly
15. ash
16. hazel

For a hand drill, I would advise you to use timber from the very top of this list as a hearth and to drill into it with either an elder, buddleia or clematis drill. If you are struggling to find a drill piece long enough, then a hollow elder rod can be tipped with one of the other woods. It is much more difficult to collect hand-drill wood from the forest to use immediately, as anyone about to embark on a fantasy survival situation, especially one involving marauding zombies, should take note.

By no means exhaustive, this list is only a guide, as inevitably there will be a huge variation within species. I have had both willow and elder so hard that it is barely possible to make an impression on them when drilling. Here, I have stuck to the species I have tried an awful lot and with which I have good experience. Moreover, mixing and matching your woods will change things a great deal: using a harder wood as the spindle to drill into a softer board may make for an easy fire, despite a wood's placement on this list.

Component Parts

Bow and String
The bow should be as light as possible, but not flexible – too much bend will cause the drill to slip in the string when pressure is brought to bear. For a beginner, an ideal length from one string nock to the other would be from the centre of their chest to their fingertips. If too short, it is difficult to get enough drill revolutions out of each stroke to build up sufficient friction; if too long, it becomes unwieldy. There is only so far you can push the bow, it is dependent on the reach of your arm, and any extra length in the bow beyond this is wasted.

You can make the bow from green wood or dry wood but bear in mind that green wood will be heavier. Despite being called a bow, it doesn't have to be excessively bent, just bowed enough to allow the drill to travel cleanly. (I find very bowed bows quite difficult to control when drilling.)

The string must be tough, particularly with regard to abrasion. I have found that good-quality paracord, chainsaw starter cord and leather all

bow drill set comprises five elements: bow and string, bearing block, ember pan, drill and hearth.

work well. It is possible to make the string from natural plant and tree fibres, but they do not last as long, so modern materials are best – at least while you're learning the technique. Do not use cord of excessive diameter: once you get up around ¼in (5mm) you will have difficulty achieving tension, and there may be too much friction between string and drill, making everything more difficult to move.

Bearing Block

The bearing block needs to be harder than the wood the drill is made from, or green wood – or in an ideal world, both. A small hole is made in this block and used to centre the top end of the drill. I find that splitting a short log 3in (8cm) or so in diameter down the centre works well. The friction really needs to be minimised here, to make the whole thing as easy to push as possible. Some people use shells to this end, but if you are going to do this, be aware that they can shatter in your hand.

Please also avoid using skateboard wheel bearings – this misses the point entirely. You might just as well use a cordless power drill, or better yet, a box of matches …

Ember Pan

The ember pan sits under the hearth board. It is there to catch the ember and insulate it from the ground. Anything dry can be used for this, from wood chips to cardboard, or even the blade of your knife. Avoid using oily barks such as birch and cherry, since they tend to roll up with the heat and smother your precious ember. In addition, avoid anything too thick, as it becomes difficult to stabilise the hearth board on top.

All the elements described above can be made using tools and techniques explained in Chapters 2 and 3.

Drill

The drill's best dimensions are a hotly debated topic. I can only share how I make them, and the reasons why. I base this on what has seemed to work best while teaching hundreds, perhaps thousands, of people the technique since 1997.

The drill should be shaped to minimise friction at the top, bearing block end, and to maximise friction at the other end. You will find that, in using the set, the non-friction end and the hole in the bearing block will wear – this can lead to the whole apparatus binding up. Therefore, it is a good idea to make the taper as long and acute as possible, to maximise the chance of keeping your drill revolving freely. I tend to start with the drill around 7–10in (30–40cm) in length, which gives me enough wood to lock it against my leg.

Diameter is another discussion, with two schools of thought. On the one hand, a large diameter gives greater surface contact and therefore more friction; on the other hand, a smaller drill gives more revolutions for each stroke and thus more friction. It is also easier to move a small drill quickly. For that reason, I am a fan of a smaller drill, somewhere between ½ and ¾in (15–20mm) in diameter; but then, I may be a woodsman set in my ways, and you might find that a different approach works better for you. (I have found that very small drills tend to bounce in the hearth and lose contact, but once I did have great success making fire with a pencil – often, they are made of cedar.)

Opposite: The drill is shaped to minimise friction at one end and maximise it at the other. The set was carved so tha the pith is in the board, where it won't cause any problems.

Hearth

The hearth board should be flat enough that it sits nicely on the ground, and wide enough to completely accept the full diameter of the drill. I usually make the board about as thick as the diameter of the drill. If you make them thicker, you have lots of cutting to do when making the notch; too thin and it is possible to drill completely through the board before you manage to make fire.

At the very least, if you do make fire on a thin hearth, you won't get many goes before you have to start a new hole. When you cut the notch, make sure the sides are parallel and don't form any kind of triangle as this can affect the shape of the ember that you produce (there are some notes on this topic below on p.253, where I discuss the fire pyramid). In addition, be sure to cut the sides as cleanly as possible, because if there are any tiny splinters, they will be apt to take the ember with the board when you roll it out of the way.

Technique

Here I will describe the construction and bowing techniques together, as it makes sense to use sound methods from the beginning to build good muscle memory.

Our initial carving should leave us with a board and drill, as illustrated, together with a non-flexing bow with string and a bearing block. An elegant way of attaching the string to the bow uses an X-cut (described in Chapter 3), with a timber hitch at one end and three or four half-hitches at the other (see Chapter 9).

1. Make a small pilot hole on the bearing block, and a second in the hearth board. These are merely to locate the respective ends of the drill. You don't have to make them very large – in fact, making them too big may cause problems.

2. Put the wood on the ground to do this, keeping your hand well out of the way, and rotate the knife away from your body to cut out a portion of the hole.

3. Move the block and repeat the process to cut out the other half. *Do not be tempted to do this task in your hand.* (I once saw someone try this, only for the bearing block to split and sever a couple of tendons.)

Adopting the Correct Stance

Aside from poor wood selection (discussed earlier) and faults in construction (which I will cover shortly), there are two main barriers to success when using a bow drill, which are easily corrected by good technique. To be avoided at all costs is the tendency for the bowstring to ride up and down, causing the drill to wobble about all over the place. Both issues can be avoided by adopting the correct stance.

The description here is based on a right-handed person and would need to be reversed if you are left-handed.

1. To place the drill in the bow, stand on the end of the bow and lay the drill at 90° across the string, with the blunt end facing to the left.

2. As you are standing on the bow you can use both hands to toggle the drill into the string. Two things should be considered: first, the string needs to be pretty tight, otherwise the drill will slip when pressure is applied; second, don't let go of the drill, otherwise it will fly out, whacking you across the knuckles in the process.

3. Try to get the drill on the outside of the string, to maximise its travel without hitting the bow.

ep your hand well away when making the pilot holes.

Putting the drill in the bow.

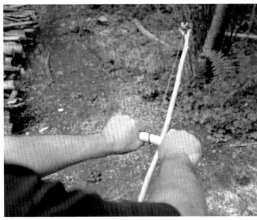

1. Place your left foot as close to the hole as possible and, with the drill almost touching your foot, bring your left hand and bearing block around the outside of your left leg.

2. Place the drill's sharp end into the bearing block and its blunt end into the hearth. Lock your wrist against your shin, as this stops the drill wobbling.

3. Ensure that your foot is far enough forward that your left leg is bent, with the centre of your chest over your toes. This allows you to put your weight onto the drill to apply pressure, rather than relying on pushing alone. Your right knee should be almost in line with the heel of your left, to give a clear passage for the bow.

4. Hold the bow right at the end and begin to bow gently, increasing pressure and speed as the set starts to bed in.

5. To prevent the bow scooping – which will cause the string to ride up – you must bow parallel to the ground. (I find this is best achieved by pushing from the shoulder, as if you are marching; this keeps your arm straight and the bow parallel. Your wrist must also be positioned to ensure the bow is level).

6. Use the full length of the bow to impart as many revolutions as possible.

Staying upright greatly aids this technique. If you lean over, you are forced to push away from the centre of your body and usually, to stop hitting the ground, the elbow bends. When applying pressure, think more of falling forwards on to the hearth, rather than just pushing. It is OK to lean your head out of the smoke, but this is not the same as leaning your whole body over.

Adopting the correct stance is vital.

Remember to start off slow and steady, as you are bedding in the set – and even though you are not applying full force, still try to maintain good posture to create the correct muscle memory. You can experiment with speed and pressure until you can hear the wood powder being ground off. You also should see copious smoke from the base of the drill. You may get lots of smoke from the top end, too. This is normal, but sometimes lubricating this end with a leaf and/or easing off the pressure will help to harden the tip, which also reduces the wear.

Cutting the Notch

At this stage, you are not actually going to make fire, as there is nowhere for your ember to form until you have cut the notch, and the notch can be made only when the hole you are making in the board exactly matches the diameter of the drill. This is best checked by looking down the end of the drill to make sure it is completely black.

Now a notch can be cut, as close to one-eighth of the diameter of the circle or dish in the hearth board as possible.

! To be certain that it is an eighth, it is imperative that you cut the notch only when the dish is the right size.

Clockwise from top left: The bottom of your drill must match the hole before you cut the notch; Gentle nibbling with the knife is the key to fine tuning the notch; Pushing down on the knife while rocking the work gives both power and control

It is also important that the notch is central and goes to the centre of the dish (the troubleshooting table below has a bit more about this).

I always cut the notch on the side of the board closest to me. This stops often wet detritus being pulled onto the ember by the bow. When cutting the notch, it is best either to nibble pieces out using a knife, or place the board on another board and press down with the knife, rocking the board at the same time. Avoid using a saw or batoning.

Creating the Ember

Once the notch has been cut, the same bow technique and position are used as for bedding in, but this time the ember pan is inserted under the notch to catch the forming coal. I am asked frequently how you know when to stop: I normally say play about with speed and pressure until you hear a grinding noise and copious smoke starts to be produced. Eventually, the smoke should start to come from the notch itself and not merely the base of the drill. Once you notice this happening, keep doing whatever you are doing for five or six seconds longer, and you should have a self-sustaining ember.

Fire needs air and hates moisture. Therefore, it is important to roll the hearth board off the ember fairly quickly. I normally hold the ember in place with a twig or my knife blade and roll the board away from me. I also lift the ember up at this stage to get it away from the damp ground. At this point, you'll have to leave the ember to coalesce: if you put it into your tinder too early, most of it will fall away, leaving a small piece of fire trying to burn a large tinder bundle. (The section on tinder on p.255 has further instructions.)

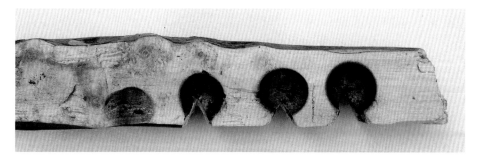

Examples of good and bad notches, from left to right: (1) the drill is too close to the edge; (2) this notch is off centre; (3) the notch doesn't reach into centre of the drill hole; and (4) a good position.

The ember.

Hand Drill

The process for a hand drill is very similar in terms of bedding in and creating a notch of sufficient proportions and position. For me, at least, I have found the most effective way to use one is to rotate the drill with the lower, fleshy parts of your hands, rather than the palms. Unless you employ thumb loops, your hands will slide down, and you must be fairly quick to get them back to the top of your drill. Delay too long and everything will have a chance of cooling down, which is a further problem that is not so prevalent when using a bow drill.

There is a technique called 'floating hands': a way of rotating the hands to stop them sliding down and thus maintaining friction between drill and

y preferred hand drill position.

hearth. Personally, I struggle to put enough downward force on using this technique but, once again, I may just be set in my ways. Many people can perform this technique sitting cross-legged. I, on the other hand, prefer to kneel over the set, using a separate stick held under my knee to brace the board. I find this a much more efficient placement of my body weight.

! When learning, you may find it beneficial to team up with a second person, swapping each time one of your hands reaches the base of the drill.

Troubleshooting for Bow and Hand Drill

Problem	Reason
Drill flies off the board	Drill not vertical String riding up due to bow scooping Drilling too close to the edge of the board, so the drill falls out Insufficient pressure Drill too short
Drill slips in string	Bow too flexible String too loose
Dust forming around the hole and not falling into the notch	Notch too narrow Notch off-centre Notch not reaching the centre Drill wobble
Notch moves	Leaning the drill away from the vertical when bowing Drill wobble
Powder is brown, not black (ember not getting hot)	Insufficient pressure Insufficient speed Poor-quality wood Inefficient technique Not using the whole length of the bow
Powder is like iron filings	Damp wood Decayed wood

Squeaking, and/or polishing of the friction end of the drill	Insufficient speed Insufficient pressure Poor-quality wood Damp wood Inefficient technique Not using the whole length of the bow
Drill is too hard to push	Hole in the bearing block is too deep Taper on the non-friction end lost Hole into board is so deep that the sides and not the tip of the drill are now rubbing String has too large a diameter

Above all, stop and correct things as you go. Don't try to push through a problem if something is not going right. It is all too easy to wear yourself out and become despondent, when all that is needed is a tiny tweak. As I mentioned at the beginning of this chapter, it is vitally important that you believe the technique will work. A friction set generally doesn't respond to being beasted into submission, but the smallest of changes can produce results.

Practise little and often, rather than attempting marathon sessions. Unless someone is there to watch your technique, when a beginner is tired it can be difficult to maintain the right stance and method and forge good muscle memory.

Establishing a Fire

Regardless of how you start your fire, be it with friction, flint and steel, or matches, there are certain stages that are best to follow to guarantee success.

It helps to think about how a fire works. Most of us will remember the 'fire triangle' from schooldays. In essence, a fire needs three things to get established: heat, oxygen and fuel. Instead, I encourage you to think of fire as a pyramid since, in addition to the elements mentioned, a fire also needs height – this is also true of the tiny ember from your bow drill, which will go out if it flattens out instead of forming a nice high coal, just as surely as it will if sweat drips on it! However, do remember that the elements making up the pyramid need to be proportional. A match, an enormous log and the outdoors are all the elements needed to make a fire, but clearly you aren't going to start one from that combination.

Coal Extenders

As the name suggests, these will take your initial heat source and make it bigger and longer lasting. Generally, they do not produce raging flames that burn sticks to ash – often, they merely glow – but they can be a real boon, especially if your tinder is slightly damp or coarse. Coal extenders include, in the main, fungi and seed heads, although when buffed very fine some inner barks can serve the purpose too.

Appropriate fungi include King Alfred's cake and horse hoof varieties, but in my experience most fungi, when dry, will hold and expand a coal. Handy seed heads include thistledown, cotton grass, bulrush and rosebay willowherb. Once again, it is worth experimenting with anything that you think might work.

Fungi are also great if you need to travel with fire: once they are established, alternatively giving and restricting their air can keep them going for ages. I once lit a *Ganoderma*, a type of bracket fungi, while doing an interview for a newspaper. I was on the top of the South Downs in the UK and walked all the way down with it still burning. In fact, I found it difficult to stamp out. The weather was very dry, and I became a little concerned, so in the end I stuffed it down a drain.

It is possible to make your own coal extenders, too. Charcloth is probably the best-known example. It is made by heating a natural textile, such as cotton, with a limited supply of air. The result is blackened cloth that takes a spark readily or makes any kind of coal bigger. I favour the cotton polishing cloths that you find in garages, as they have a very open weave that stays open when converted to charcoal. This means that it catches sparks readily. (For an idea of how to do this, see charcoal-making in Chapter 7.)

Accelerants

Again, as the name suggests, these cause a fire to burn hotter and faster. They are not always great at starting a blaze but work brilliantly on boosting a weak fire. There are several man-made accelerants that will be familiar to most campers: the most common are petroleum jelly and candle wax. From the natural world, resins from conifers can be used to the same end – often, they can be collected from damaged areas of bark, as the resin drips down the main trunk.

In my region, many conifers suffer from butt rot, and they snap in high winds, just at the point where the rot stops. The wood there is packed with great stuff, as are the branch knots found on fallen and partially decayed pines. Any wood packed with unusual amounts of resin is called 'fat wood'. In deciduous forests, the outer bark of birch and cherry contain oil, providing both fuel in the form of bark and an accelerant in the form of this oil. Again, experimentation is the key, as some species may yield far more than others.

Tinder

Tinder is the big bundle of nest-like material that can be seen smoking merrily away in many a promotional shot for bushcraft schools. It can come from a variety of sources and, in many cases, be prepared so finely that it will light from a tiny spark and certainly from the coal produced by a bow drill.

If the weather is especially inclement (welcome to England!), do feel free to pack the centre of the bundle liberally with any dry coal extender of your choice. If things just aren't happening, don't be shy about dripping resin over your tiny flame before it finally splutters and goes out, taking all possibility of hot soup with it.

It's worth offering a few words on making the bundle at this stage, as many people make their tinder bundles too loose. You need to blow tinder into flame with many methods of initiating a fire, but you certainly must do so if you are using a bow drill coal.

It is important that you make the cup in your tinder bundle (see the next section) only after you have first hard-packed the material. It is all too easy to blow the hard-won ember straight out of the bottom of a loosely gathered bundle and onto the damp ground. Use the bird's nest as a model for your bundle, secure enough that the wee ones can't fall through (except, of course, nests of wood pigeons, who frankly build rubbish nests and should have a word with themselves).

A properly packed bundle of tinder.

I break tinder materials down into their four main sources, as follows.

Inner Bark

These are the phloem layer of a tree (see Chapter 5). Many species produce this material in sheets that, when fresh, can be used for craftwork. When dry, this material can be buffed up into tinder. All tinder trees are potential craft trees in this regard. They include:

- elm
- Lawson's cypress
- Leyland cypress

- ☐ lime
- ☐ sweet chestnut
- ☐ sycamore
- ☐ western red cedar
- ☐ willow.

This isn't an exhaustive list, of course, and if you experiment, you may well find others in quantity in your own region. A few different approaches can be taken to processing inner bark, depending on the state it is in. (Again, for these, see Chapter 5.)

Outer Bark
Outer bark can also be used and is found in relative abundance on species such as clematis and honeysuckle. However, honeysuckle is quite tricky to get very fine, as it can only really be pulled apart, so it is best used with a coal extender inside – the coarser the material, the harder it is to light.

! (When harvesting, be careful not to tear into the living part of the plant.)

Birch and Cherry Bark
It is worth mentioning these at this point, even though they fall outside the general tinder group. They will light from sparks if you use fine, paper-like pieces, but I avoid them for heat sources such as charcloth and friction fire embers, as they tend to curl up around the ember when they get hot and put it out.

However, these barks are great as a fire-starter in their own right. A big fistful won't need any extra help setting fire to your kindling.

! Take care when removing the material, only taking what the tree is naturally shedding. With cherry, I tend to cut off these peeling pieces, as invariably they tear into the tree itself when you pull on them.

Herbaceous Materials
There is a great deal of room for experimentation within this final group, and I have used everything from dry bracken to cleavers. Anything dry is worth a go, although undoubtedly some will produce finer material than others.

A range of fire-lighting options.

I use dry grass frequently when teaching and demonstrating, partly because it is an easy, abundant and relatively non-destructive way of getting lots of tinder. I also use grass because it can be hard to get the thing burning and is therefore a great teaching aid (although some of my students may disagree). The point is that if you can get this going, then working on other materials is easy.

If you do want to try it yourself, you can buy grass (hay) as pet bedding. Just be sure you get the uncut stuff, as it holds together better.

Blowing up a Tinder Bundle

When trying to get your tinder to take, common mistakes are blowing too hard and failing to squash fuel into the ember as it grows. To help you avoid these errors, I will give a rough description of the process of turning your hard-won coal into fire. My account focuses on a friction ember, but the method applies equally to any coal-like material you might use.

- Prepare your bundle with a shallow cup but in a base that's packed solid, so you are blowing the ember into the fuel. The bundle should be the size of a grapefruit as a good average but increase this in bad weather.

wing a bundle into fire.

- Slide your fully coalesced coal from the ember pan into the cup. If you have waited long enough, the ember should still be in a big lump and not fall apart.

- Get your fingertips level with the ember and the ember at eye level.

- Blow gently on it, but with sustained breath. If you start to make an odd spitting noise, you are blowing too hard; if you see sparks flying, you are shattering the ember.

- As the heat grows, squeeze in gently with your fingers, otherwise you will merely burn a hole in the middle of the bundle.

- If you start to hyperventilate, stop and gently waft the bundle to get air through it. Don't do this until you are happy that the fire is becoming established.

- Once it flames, invert it to allow the flames to travel up through the rest of your bundle. Place it on your fire site.

The process described is probably the worst-case scenario. With many types of tinder, especially when used with a coal extender, getting to flames is fairly straightforward and liberties can be taken.

Feather Sticks

Feather sticks can replace both tinder and kindling, or just one of these elements. They can be used with splints that are split off from the same sort of wood from which they are made. Alternatively, kindling can be placed on top, and the curls used as tinder. They work well as a base from which to start a star fire or a 'V' fire (see p.271).

Opposite: A feather-stick f

Siting a Fire

Controversially, but in many ways sensibly, you need the landowner's permission to light a fire. In addition, you should always think about how to minimise your impact on the land.

I remember visiting some woodland a few years back. It was the very place I'd had my first experience of camping under trees, as well as one of the first woods I had ever explored properly, in which I'd spent long periods. I would almost say I grew up among those trees. My friends and I swam in the lake there, found deer and badger tracks, caught newts and generally wandered around having huge wilderness fantasies, humming the theme tune to *Grizzly Adams* (people of a certain age will remember that show!).

I took my wife back there, many years after my last youthful visit, to find a changed place. Fire scars were everywhere, complete with beer cans and general detritus. It is hard to envisage a youngster being able to conjure their own *Grizzly Adams*-style wilderness fantasy with quite the same force. Imagination is so vital to inspiring people to realise their dreams that we must allow visitors to experience these special places on as blank a canvas as possible, to stimulate it.

Fire siting, then, is about common sense damage limitation, which can be easily done if following a few essential pointers.

- Don't light your fire under hanging branches. There is never any need to scorch leaves and kill the boughs of trees.

- Don't set any fire too close to the trunks of trees. These too can be damaged.

- Don't burn roots, as damaging living roots can cause health problems for the tree, perhaps years later. Beware of setting fire to dead roots or stumps: the fire may spring back into life, long after you have moved on.

- Don't set a fire amid deep leaf litter, especially conifer needles. These also can smoulder and flare up long after the event.

- Don't make your fire on heavy organic matter, such as peat. Again, these fires can start up, and often in a different location, as fire can travel underground.

- Don't destroy surrounding ground vegetation: there is no need to light your fire in the middle of a patch of wildflowers or grasses, for example.

- Don't light a fire on glassy rocks such as flint, or on rocks that have been in water for years. They often explode, with alarming results.

- Don't create a conflagration that's fierce enough to burn a few dozen heretics when all you want is a cup of tea.

- Don't start a fire before clearing leaf litter back to the soil over an area at least twice as big as you think the fire will need.

- Don't surround your fire with rocks – all that happens is you discolour a previously naturally coloured object.

Fire Platforms

The UK can be a pretty wet old place, so scraping back leaf litter frequently reveals damp soil on which no self-respecting fire would ever consider establishing itself. Therefore, it is useful to site your fire on a platform, which should comprise dry, firewood-quality sticks, laid tightly parallel to each other so the ground cannot be seen underneath. The effect is insulation of the fire from the ground, while elevating it slightly to allow good airflow and, eventually, providing fuel.

Lighting feather sticks on a decent platform, with the leaf litter cleared away.

If the ground is especially wet, a double- or even triple-layer platform will lift the fire even further. In some conditions – including wet ground – it can be advantageous to use green wood as a platform to prevent it burning, which would turn your hard-won fire into a smoking hole in the ground. By contrast, during a baking hot summer, it is usually possible to skip the platform and light your fire straight onto the ground.

Fuel

Before going to the bother of starting a fire, you should make sure that you have all your fuel graded and ready to go. Start with very fine kindling. This needs to be very small in diameter and as dry as can be found. Collect two good-sized bundles – they should resemble a couple of besoms, or witch's brooms, and be about as long. If these are only slightly thicker than a match at their thinnest point, that's a great start.

Next, grab a load of small sticks, maybe as thick as your finger. Work your way up with different bundles until you reach your main fuel size,

bearing in mind that you don't necessarily need huge-diameter firewood for a picnic in the local woods. Separating these bundles out makes life much easier later.

If this seems overcomplicated, it could be because it is aimed at building a fire that has been lit from a tinder bundle. No doubt you could jump a few grades in fuel size if you're starting with a huge wad of cotton soaked in a tub of petroleum jelly. However, if the chips are down and you really need a fire, then going back to the systematic gathering and preparation of fuel wood should ensure success.

Size-graded fuel, ready to go.

To repeat, firewood needs to be as dry as possible, and those twigs found resting off the ground will be more likely to fit the bill. Make sure they are dead and snap cleanly. If you have to twist a small diameter twig into odd shapes just to get it to break, it is likely to be too green. Remember that trees can be dead without being long dead.

Experiment also with different species. Hard, dense timber often burns with great heat, but may not produce a lot of light. Adding some lighter woods such as birch to the mix can make for a cheerier camp. (Showing my age, we used to use the name of the long-defunct airline BOAC as an acronym for the best firewood: Beech, Oak, Ash and Chestnut, to which you can add hornbeam. There are also several versions of the poem 'Logs to Burn' by Honor Goodhart, which is a great start when selecting firewood (I have included at the end of this chapter another in this vein by Lady Celia Congreve, 'The Firewood Poem').

Ignition

Remember the concept that fire needs the all-important pyramid of ingredients to be successful? Assuming that you are outdoors, have nice, dry, appropriately sized fuel and a source of ignition, all you need to remember is the height aspect – this is where the two tightly packed bundles of twigs come in.

- Light your tinder – be it from a bow drill ember, or curls of birch bark – and place it, burning, on your platform.

- Grab the two bundles, one in each hand, and hold them one on top of another, with the point where they cross over the flaming tinder. (This is why we leave them long: it means you can avoid major burns. By holding the bundles, you can experiment with the height, holding them slightly off the heat or placing them closer, as required.)

- Once alight, they can be released, and the progressive grades of fuel wood added. (I tend towards arranging the subsequent fuel like a tightly packed star fire; see below.)

1. Create two bundles.
2. Compress them.
3. Light the fire, using waxed paper in this case.
4. Long twigs equal greater safety and control.

Fire Lays and Management

There are lots of versions of fire lays to be found, but it seems to me that they are mostly one of four basic patterns, slightly adapted. I suppose a fifth version would be the tepee fire, which often is illustrated as a way of lighting a fire: tinder is placed in the centre, then sticks are leant into each other, effectively locking everything together in a twig cone. This gives all the pyramid requirements discussed earlier and, in theory, should make an easy fire. Often, this is indeed the case.

However, in my experience, the cone either falls over or locks up totally, allowing the tinder to burn out in the middle, and the fire to die. When used as a main fire lay with bigger fuel, it burns extremely hot and bright, but eats through firewood. (All very well for Guy Fawkes night or your effigy-dispatching celebration of choice, but for me, having to get up every five minutes to put more wood on gets a little tedious, so I tend to avoid this one. However, these things are best experienced directly, so do make up your own mind.)

There always will be a trade-off between the effort expended in gathering, preparing and managing a fire and what you get back from it. For this reason, I much prefer to light a fire using either twigs or feather sticks, then turn it into the type of fire I need. Once that fire has served its purpose, it is a simple matter to change it once more. The following are what I regard as the four key fire-lay patterns.

Star Fire

The star or hunter's fire has its main fuel radiating out from the central point, like spokes from a wheel. The wheel can contain just a few spokes or be filled, depending on preference. The star fire's main advantage is the minimal preparation needed to collect firewood: if you can carry it to the fire and drop the end into the centre, or allow the fire to burn it in half, this is all the preparation required. Because it is only burning the ends of the logs, it is massively fuel efficient too (I have had four good-sized logs last for a whole week's camping).

Bear in mind that the more spokes you use, the further back the fire will spread. It will be hotter and brighter, which means using more wood. Sometimes, a shallow dish can be excavated under the central point to cut the wind and further increase fuel efficiency. However, if you make this too deep, your logs may overhang the heart of the fire and not burn very well.

A star or hunter fire.

The downside to this fire is that it is high maintenance. Without constant pushing in and restacking of logs to maintain height, the fire soon burns out. It is not a good one to be left for any period of time.

Criss-Cross Fire

The criss cross fire consists of alternate rows of parallel sticks, laid close enough together to touch. It is like several alternating platforms, laid one on top of another. Its purpose is to produce an even bed of hot coals – charcoal, in other words. Designed for cooking, it is, in essence, a barbecue.

The idea is that even-diameter timber should be used, so that it will all burn at roughly the same rate. If you mix the sizes, then some of your wood will be ash and some smouldering logs, and you'll never get the even bed you're after. If your sticks are different lengths, it is very difficult to keep them balanced without collapsing and rolling off the fire.

A criss-cross fire burnt to embers.

A criss-cross fire.

It should be possible to stand a pan on a criss-cross fire in the early stages before it turns to charcoal. While it is a great cooking fire, using it for a general campfire is impractical, due to the preparation and the fact that it burns through wood at a great rate. (I often use a criss-cross to start the brew on a wet morning, then turn it into a hunter's fire just as the kettle boils. Purely for the adoration and delight of my fellow campers, as they emerge from their tents, you understand!)

Parallel Fire

Parallel fire lays may be familiar to many as the classic wilderness long-log fire, designed to heat the whole of the body and burn for several hours. These consist of long logs lying side-by-side and stacked into a rough triangle. Between three and five sticks, depending on diameter, tend to work well.

On a smaller scale, these fires are good for grilling and cooking on a spit. I have used versions of different sizes to heat rocks for outdoor steam baths too. They make a great alternative to the tepee fire for a good old 'Ging Gang Goolie' singsong, as they are much more fuel efficient, yet throw out a lot of heat. Often, they do need pegging to stop the logs rolling out, and big ones can be too hot to get close enough for cooking.

There are variations of this kind of fire: a reflector can be added just behind the long log, about an arm's length, that will throw heat back towards you or your shelter; alternatively, a reflector can be built up against the fire and allowed to catch it, creating a flaming grill – an arrangement known as a 'back wall fire'.

On a small scale, this can be used for cooking. In fact, I have suspended whole chickens in front of this arrangement on wire. On a larger scale they are extremely hot, almost too hot. The back wall can be propped by driving stakes into the ground at an angle, although eventually they will burn through. Using less-seasoned wood for the wall can slow this process down a little.

If using it within a shelter, keep the logs about an arm's length away, to be fairly easy to reach and fiddle with, but not so close as to be unsafe. Moreover, bear in mind that if you double the distance between you and a fire, you will be four times colder.

This long-log fire has been adapted into a back-wall fire.

'V' or Fan Fire

This is a great fire for bad weather, or times when low maintenance is key. The fuel is stacked in a 'V' formation to give the all-important height, then the centre of the 'V' is filled in. It is a fire for exposed places with constant wind: beaches are a great example. The idea is that the point of the 'V' is downwind and, in the situation already described, this arrangement stops the fire from migrating. Because there is no fuel beyond the point, the fire can't go anywhere. (Anyone who has lit a fire on a windy day and found it moved 6ft [1.82m] will appreciate the value of this.)

A further advantage of this arrangement is its self-feeding nature: the formation can be stacked as high as your fuel store allows, and will constantly drop down into the fire, which – so long as the wind remains constant – is relatively small. I once built one in appalling conditions, using fairly big logs and as high as my waist, as I had to leave camp for a few hours. The fire was still burning well on my return. The physical arrangement of the fuel means that the wood above is kept warm and dry before it hits the fire.

erybody loves a good 'V' or fan fire.

There is an old expression that the best way to cool down a fire is to put more wood on it. This is presumably because energy from the fire is needed to convert the new fuel. This fire is more efficient in this regard. On a small scale, it is a fine way to start a fire. To this end, it can be built with tinder in the 'V' point, and pre-laid prior to lighting.

Leave No Trace

Clearing up is an integral part of fire lighting, and there are a couple of approaches to take. You may choose first to spend time ensuring that as much of the charred remains of your fire have been burnt, leaving the minimum to dispose of solid stuff. If you are planning to come back to the same spot, it may be worth storing the larger pieces (if properly cooled) for future use. In either case, go through the following process to leave no trace:

- Use water and a stick to mix your fire into a sludge, to extinguish it properly. Of course, you can just let the fire go out.

- Pass your hand a few centimetres above the fire site to test for hot spots. If you find any, irrigate them as above.

- Gently use your hands instead of the stick to mix the sludge around. The idea is that it should all feel stone cold at this stage.

- When you're happy that the fire is not only out but cold, you can begin to scatter handfuls to the four winds. Scrape the sludge right back to the soil level.

- When it has completely gone, cover over with the leaf litter that you scraped back to lay your platform.

earing away the fire site.

should be hard to detect where the fire was —
ave no trace.

If you think the fire has been exceptionally hot, then spiking holes in the ground to encourage water to cool deeper may be considered.

The overall idea is to make it very hard to spot where the fire was and to avoid changing the soil balance of the area – this encourages plants such as nettles, which don't normally grow in such locations, to appear.

The Firewood Poem

Beechwood fires are bright and clear
If the logs are kept a year,
Chestnut's only good they say,
If for logs 'tis laid away.
Make a fire of Elder tree,
Death within your house will be;
But ash new or ash old,
Is fit for a queen with crown of gold.

Birch and fir logs burn too fast,
Blaze up bright and do not last,
it is by the Irish said,
Hawthorn bakes the sweetest bread.
Elm wood burns like churchyard mould,
E'en the very flames are cold.
But ash green or ash brown
is fit for a queen with golden crown.

Poplar gives a bitter smoke,
Fills your eyes and makes you choke,
Apple wood will scent your room,
Pear wood smells like flowers in bloom.
Oaken logs, if dry and old
keep away the winter's cold.
But ash wet or ash dry,
a king shall warm his slippers by.

(Lady Celia Congreve)

7

Glue, Dye, Ink and Charcoal

My early experiences with glue made specifically from trees were not, perhaps, the cleanest a person could have. Black, oozing pitch can be a fickle beast and difficult to manage. However, if used appropriately, it does create some of the finest free glue to be found in nature.

Sealing the bindings for arrow or spear points is a perfect example of when pitch glues come into their own. However, as I found out, trying to put fletching on arrow shafts is not. If made correctly, pitch glue is thermoplastic: it requires a heat source to make it pliable and adhesive. You can imagine how sticking three separate feathers on a skinny hazel wand is more likely to leave the craftsman tarred and feathered and holding a fairly unsuitable arrow. Mind you, it does bring to mind an old joke: 'What is brown and sticky? A stick.'

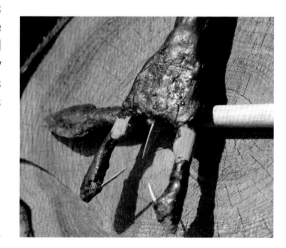

Resin-based glue in action.

Glue

Perhaps the best-known source of glue from trees is conifer resin. This can be found dripping from wounds in branches and from the damaged bark of many coniferous trees, notably pine and spruce. Once in contact with air, the resin gradually hardens with a whitish crust. It is very brittle and, although it can be heated to make it pliable again, it will always dry into a brittle state, which makes it unsuitable for most applications. For example, if conifer resin is used to secure the points of arrows or to seal containers to make them waterproof, the slightest shock or impact causes it to shatter.

For this reason, it is best tempered slightly by adding more pliable material. Either charcoal, beeswax or a blend of both are used most frequently, although animal dung has also been employed. Getting the right combination is not an exact science, especially when done in a rustic setting. Heat is used in the manufacture of glues of this type, so it is inevitable that some of the resin will evaporate, in fact, beeswax also evaporates. This makes hitting on exact proportions problematic.

I tend to aim for a 50/50 mix of resin to temper, with beeswax and or charcoal my preferred medium. However, the proportions are slightly more critical here: use too much wax and on a hot day the glue will drip from your craft project and no longer hold the pieces in place.

The plus side is that nothing is wasted: if your mix is too plastic, add more resin; if too brittle, add more temper. It is also worth experimenting with adding vegetable fibre to increase flexibility – rabbit droppings would be a good start.

Collecting Resin

Scraping

At the most basic level, scraping resin from one of the areas described above will achieve results. However, it is a little messy and certainly not a job for your best knife, as everything is liable to be covered with sticky gunk. Throughout this book we are considering tasks that can be done with a minimum of equipment. With this in mind, resin can be simply melted on a hot rock, tilted slightly to allow the liquid to flow. Any impurities in the resin – and there are bound to be some, especially bits of bark – can be flicked away with a stick.

Examples of resin collecting around damaged areas.

Glue stick.

Heating resin on a rock.

I favour a rock with a slight depression into which the fluid can be diverted, then mixed with the temper. When you are happy with the results, the liquid glue can be picked up on the end of the stick. Alternatively, dipping the stick into the mix and allowing it to cool produces a glue stick toffee apple. I like to think this would be standard-issue kit for a journeying ancestor: the thermoplastic nature of the substance would allow him or her to make running repairs on their hunting-and-gathering equipment.

A slightly more sophisticated process would involve collecting the resin and melting it through a sieve. This could be made simply by banging small holes in the bottom of a can with a nail or something similar. Again, the object is to leave behind any impurities and allow pure resin to drip through the holes once it has been heated into a liquid state.

Dry Distillation
Larger quantities can be collected and purified through dry distillation. Effectively, this is making charcoal (which is covered at the end of this chapter), but instead of the charcoal being the final product, all the stuff that comes off the charcoal is the goal.

- Sit one tin can with a lid on top of a second can without a lid.

- Punch a small hole in the first can, to allow the resin to drip through into the second.

- Pack the top tin with finely split splints of conifer wood. (Birch bark can be treated in the same way to produce birch tar, which is also used to seal and bind.)

- Then, bury the collection tin in the ground up to its rim, and sit the now-filled top tin on this, so that the hole faces down. It is possible to find tins that fit very tightly together if you're prepared to hunt around a bit.

Clockwise from right: Ready to be part buried and fired; A double tin – one has a hole to collect oils; Fill the top tin with birch bark or conifer splints; After firing, the bark is reduced to charcoal; Tar or oil can be produced, depending on how much it is reduced.

- Now, kindle a fire on top of and around this tin. As the wood or bark is converted into charcoal, everything is driven off, leaving behind mostly carbon. The by-products of the charcoal process, including resin, sap and water, now flow through the hole into the collecting tin. How long this takes depends very much on the quality of your fire: it could be done in as little as twenty minutes, or it may take much longer.

- Once all the material, be that bark or wood, has turned to charcoal, the process is finished, and no further liquid will be obtained. It isn't really a problem if the process is stopped too early, as the tin can be re-sited at any point and fired again.

! It is important to remember that the liquid is highly flammable, so before removing the top be sure to clear away all traces of fire.

What is left in the tin may be quite liquid – when it comes from birch bark it is often referred to as 'Russian oil', which was widely used as a preservative for wood and leather. To make the liquid more viscous, it can be gently heated to evaporate excess fluid. When finished it is usually fairly plastic, so tempering may not be needed – it may help firm up the mixture though. (Birch oil is used also as a base for insect repellent, although I'm not convinced that I would want to put too much of it on my skin. It is rich in powerful chemicals, including phenols, which you might wish only to apply with caution.)

Natural Dyes and Inks

The Process

Whole books can be written – and, indeed, have been written – about natural dyeing (see the Further Reading section). For the purposes of this book, I will describe the simplest process that still achieves results. Like so many of the subjects described here, it is possible to go to a higher and deeper level.

The basic principle is to take a bunch of tree material (which may be bark, leaves, fruit or roots), damage it a little by breaking it up, then leave it in warm water for as long as possible to extract the pigments. This may involve spending some time listening to the radio while you check pans gently steaming on the kitchen cooker; it may involve frantically manning a fire in the wind and rain. Either way, you must keep this process going for as long as you possibly can – at the very least until you have coloured the water.

The material that you plan to dye can now be placed in the pan and left. You might get a result after only a short time, but it is better to leave the material at least overnight. Some people insist on removing the plant material prior to this, some don't bother – I suggest you find out what works best for you.

It is fun to experiment with different materials, since they take colour in different ways. Try with some spare wool, cotton and linen as a start, before you start work on your best and favourite T-shirt.

All sorts of projects are possible using natural dyes.

Mordants and Modifiers

Mordants

The word 'mordant' comes from the French verb *mordre*, meaning 'to bite'. Mordants are mineral salts that bind dyes into fibre. They are added to the material to help fix the colour, otherwise with use – especially washing – the dye simply runs out of the material after a relatively short time.

Some mordants can be added before the material enters its dye bath, some can be added to the bath while dyeing is occurring, and some are

Clockwise from right:
Walnut husk and ash.
Alder.
Walnut.
Amelanchier, with a few pieces that missed
the dye bath but showing the contrast.
Sycamore.
Goat willow.
Sweet chestnut.

added after the material has been dyed. Many chemicals are used as mordants, but probably the easiest to find is common salt. Tannin is another possibility: it occurs naturally in many areas of the tree, especially bark. This means that, although it may not be the case if you are using dye made from fruit, leaves and flowers, certainly for dyes from most tree species, mordants are not required.

I tend to pre-mordant with salt anyway. To be honest, if you do this and then find that the solution is rich in tannin – well, all that has happened is that you've wasted a bit of salt. I don't believe it will affect the colour very much. To use salt, simply make a salt solution using warm water and steep your material in it until it is soaked through. I don't worry too much about specific proportions, just make it salty.

However, in reality, it is very difficult to make natural dye truly colour fast using rustic techniques.

Modifiers

Modifiers can be mordants or stand-alone chemicals, although strictly speaking, a modifier is not considered strong enough in its own right to be a mordant. However, modifiers can alter the colour of the dye bath, sometimes quite dramatically. This is another area where it is fun to experiment a bit, since you can get some startling results fairly quickly.

Other Factors Affecting Dye Colours/Strengths

In addition to modifiers, there are a number of other factors to bear in mind that might not occur initially to the would-be dyer but can affect the colour achieved through any natural dyeing process. If you are dyeing commercially, this is perhaps a bigger concern than for those of us who are just playing around a little with trees – nonetheless, here are a few things to note when seeking to obtain consistent colours.

Factors that cause variations when using natural dyes include the following:

- Season: vegetation contains different amounts of chemicals, including pigments, at different times of the year.

- Timing: how much contact time the material has with the dye bath.

- Temperature: how hot the dye bath is. It is possible to have the liquid too cold to release pigments, or so hot that the pigments are boiled off.

- Quantity: more dye material usually equates to a stronger solution, which may well give a deeper colour.

- Water: some dyes are sensitive to the pH of the water.

- Mordant: some mordants may modify the colour obtained.

- Dyeing vessel: stainless steel is the most neutral material you can use. Dying in other containers may result in variations of colour that may or may not be desired.

Ideas for Further Experimentation

All trees – their roots, bark, fruit and leaves – are worth trying for their potential as sources of natural dye, although it must be said that most natural dyes tend to be variations on shades of green or brown. Here are some to try, and the colours they typically produce:

- alder bark – yellow/orange
- Amelanchier berries – purple
- blackberries – purple
- blackberry roots – orange
- chestnut bark – brown
- oak bark – tan
- oak galls – black
- sycamore bark – red/orange
- walnut husks – brown/beige
- willow bark – orange.

Willow bark is an interesting one, and a good place to start, as the outer scraping from bark work can be used for dye. It also provides a great illustration of how to use a modifier. If willow is made into dye as described above, the colour is a lovely orange or perhaps a bit reddish. However, if the material and dye are boiled with a couple of handfuls of wood ash,

Willow mixed with wood ash makes a purple dye.

Dyeing bark strips to use for modifier weaving.

the colour becomes a vivid purple. The strips obtained for weaving (as described in Chapter 5) can be dyed purple using this method. You could do something similar with chestnut, but the bark of a chestnut tree goes a beautiful brown all by itself, particularly if you wet it and allow it to dry a couple of times.

Inks

Inks are essentially thick, gloopy dyes – although as they may not have to be exposed to weathering by the elements, they are less reliant on the addition of mordants. Inks can be broken down, at least when we are considering trees, into those made with tannin or berry inks.

My favourite example of the use of natural ink is the Julius Work Calendar, which dates back to Saxon times and documents a year in the life of our agricultural ancestors. The ink that this document was written with is made from the marble galls sometimes found on an oak tree. It is fascinating to think about how this ink managed to survive the ravages of time. (There are many images of this calendar online.)

Various inks from berry and tannin sources.

arble galls on an oak tree.

Ink from Tannin

Don't worry too much if you cannot find marble galls, acorns also work very well as do Knopper galls, in my experience. I have also made good ink using the husks of walnut fruit (which, as mentioned previously, works well as a dye too).

Before you think about processing the galls or acorns, get some iron vinegar solution on the go. This is pretty much essential for tannin-based inks, acting as a kind of mordant. It certainly darkens the colour of your ink almost immediately, like a little touch of alchemy.

It's very easy to make iron vinegar: just dump any rusty old items you have about the place – old hinges, nails, whatever else – into a jar of malt vinegar and leave it. You can leave it for days or weeks – in many ways, the longer you leave it, the better – but you can get a passable result in a relatively short time.

I'm sure you would get more consistent results by using measured ingredients, but I prefer simply to mix a few things together and see what happens, so we're just going to gather a couple of good handfuls of acorns and/or marble galls and boil them up. The galls, in particular, benefit from being bashed a little first to crush them. (Incidentally, it is worth noting that I have made ink with a much smaller amount of material than I just described.)

- Boiling should begin to turn the water a darker colour almost immediately: this is the tannin being released. You can boil this solution for hours or days, but once the change in the colour of the water is noticeable, you have something to work with.

- When you have something that you feel may work, strain off the solid material to leave only coloured liquid. (If you are using acorns, don't throw them away, you might want to eat them now that you've removed much of the tannin.)

- At this point, add the iron vinegar solution. Once again, try experimenting with the amounts until you achieve a good result. As a rule of thumb, five teaspoons for every litre of solution should be about right.

The final ingredient required for tannin-based ink is a binder. Its purpose is to keep the pigment suspended in the solution; it also thickens the ink. Traditionally, this was made from gum arabic, which is obtained from acacia trees, but several other substances can be used. Perhaps the most easily obtained is gelatin, which can be dissolved in hot water and added to the solution in the same proportions as the vinegar.

Ink from Berries
Several kinds of berry can be used to make inks and it is well worth exploring different possibilities for yourself. I have had a good deal of success with blackberry, which is perhaps obvious, but I have also produced a very strong purple ink using Amelanchier berries.

1. Crushed marble galls (see previous page).
2. Boiled up galls.
3. The liquid remaining after the solid material has been strained off.
4. The jar in the middle contains the ink after the iron vinegar and gelatin solutions have been added.

- You may find that better results are obtained if you freeze the berries first: it seems that breaking the fruit's cell walls with ice crystals releases more pigment.

- Once they are thoroughly thawed out, take your fruit and crush it, then squeeze out the juice using a cloth filter such as a jelly bag. (You may find that you need to boil the mixture slightly to release the maximum amount of liquid.)

- Add the iron vinegar solution, as described for the tannin-based inks, and in roughly the same proportions as above, but also add salt – because we are now using material that will effectively go off, the salt will act as a preservative. A couple of teaspoons of salt per litre should be more than enough to complete your ink.

...me berries produce spectacular colours.

Charcoal

Charcoal can be considered a by-product of producing tar and resin from trees such as spruce and birch, but also you can make it on purpose using the very same method. You simply heat wood with a limited supply of oxygen, which prevents total combustion. This can be done in huge ring kilns, efficient retorts, galvanised dustbins or an old biscuit tin.

The same technique is used to produce charcloth, which is just charcoal made from natural fibres, and is a great coal extender for lighting fires (see Chapter 6). Natural materials that have been charred once already attract fire like a magnet. There is a complicated scientific reason for this – but for now, just think that if it has been burnt once, it can burn again.

1. Pack the container with node-free willow.
2. Place it on the fire and watch as the smoke changes.
3. Plug the hole and allow the tin to cool.
4. Create a masterpiece.

Part of this burning efficiency is due to having driven off from the wood or cloth nearly everything that isn't carbon. This means that all the energy from the fire can now go into combustion rather than heating solids, gases and liquids. It also means that the material is much lighter to transport, which no doubt was part of the attraction in times gone by. The word 'collier' originally referred to charcoal burners, with the use of wood and charcoal as a prime fuel pre-dating coal by a long time. When transporting fuel out of the forest, it certainly would have made sense to focus on the lightest and most efficient forms – and if you think about burning fuel before the days of chimneys, the less smoky attributes of charcoal would have been a real boon.

Making Artist's Charcoal
The method described here produces a moderate amount of artist's charcoal or barbecue charcoal. The process involves enjoyably big fires, although it is perfectly possible to make artist's charcoal in your oven at home.

For this, willow is traditionally the tree of choice, although you may wish to experiment with others. Try to find straight, knot-free stems, otherwise you might find that your charcoal breaks at the point where the knots occurred. Incidentally, on small-diameter twigs, the area where buds and branches appear is known as a node, with the bits between referred to as internodes. For this project, we need straight, primary growth with long internodes since the finished charcoal will mirror the wood from which it was made.

Perhaps the easiest way to make charcoal is to place wood in a container and build the fire around it. Traditional ring kilns have the fire inside the vessel, but this method involves burning some of the potential charcoal to fuel the process. There will be significantly less wastage if the fire is external to the kiln although, of course, you are still burning wood to fuel the external fire.

Punching a hole through the container is important, since it allows the release of excess gas (and excess gas is no fun in any situation). It also gives you an indication of when the process is finished – as all the volatile oils and water are released from the wood, there is a lot of thick white smoke.

I remember reading somewhere years ago that in the region of 90 per cent of smoke is water vapour. Therefore, it is possible to tell the quality of your firewood by the amount of smoke that it produces. As the process of charcoal-making progresses, the smoke becomes thinner and less white.

Eventually, it will turn blue, become very sparse and then, finally, a kind of mirage heat haze is all that can be seen from the vent.

Some people stop the process only when the smoke has gone blue. I try to stop the process just before this point, because waiting that long generally means that some of your charcoal has been consumed. It may be that with charcloth or wood there is some unburnt material left in the kiln. This can be either reburnt or used to light the next fire: in my days as a charcoal burner, these were referred to as 'brown ends'.

If you close down the process too soon, don't worry, just put the whole lot back on the fire for a little longer. To close down the process, simply remove the container from the fire and plug the hole.

! Only open the vessel when it has cooled down completely. Aside from the obvious possibility of burning yourself, if you put the container in the back of your car still warm, it may well start burning halfway through your journey home.

8

Foliage, Features and Fungi

Something I really enjoyed learning when I was training as an arborist was a concept that has become known as 'the body language of trees'. In essence, it uses certain visible features to tell you about what is likely to be going on within the internal structure of a tree.

As well as enabling you to assess potential weaknesses and threats to the camper, student of bushcraft or tree feller, considering how trees respond to light and wind, in particular, can help the weary traveller find their way. This also may be true of other organisms that regard a tree as home.

In my early years as a woodsman, this would have been particularly useful on one occasion when I was felling a large willow. Unbeknown to me, the swelling at the base of the tree concealed a large hollow or cavity. I put in my sink cut as normal and was walking around the tree to cut the back when it fell over on its own. As is typical of these situations, I had an audience of experienced woodsmen on hand to enjoy the spectacle. If I were of a suspicious nature, I could almost imagine that they knew what was about to happen and had formed an orderly queue.

A veteran tree.

The purpose of this chapter is to help you to identify common trees that have been already discussed and suggested for some of the projects in this book. It is not my intention to provide a comprehensive field guide, but hopefully it will help you along the road to being able to identify common trees (see the Further Reading section). It should also help you acquire some knowledge about what those trees can used for.

I have included some common fungi associated specifically with trees as well, in the hope that should you stumble across them during woodland wanderings you will be able to identify, use or just admire them. Finally, I have discussed some common features found on trees that may keep you safe when felling, prompt interesting craft projects, or even point you in the direction of home.

Ten Trees Every Woodsman Should Know

Ash (Fraxinus excelsior)

This is a tremendously useful tree that is, unfortunately, at the time of writing, under threat due to ash dieback (caused by the fungus *Hymenoscyphus fraxineus*), which seems to be sweeping the country. Ash is identified very easily: at first glance, it seems to have many leaves. In fact, in botanical terms, a leaf is only classed as such if it has a bud at the point where the leaf stalk meets the branch. Closer inspection reveals that ash is made up of several leaflets in pairs, arranged along the leaf stalk. This means that at some point in history, a single giant leaf decided to split itself into several leaflets. This type of structure is referred to as a 'compound leaf'.

The real key to identifying this tree is its black, sometimes brown, buds, especially the terminal bud – the one at the very end of the twigs. Often, this has been described as looking like a bishop's hat.

There is good deal of folklore attached to this tree, but perhaps that should wait for another book. For now, it is enough to know that this tree has been useful for any work requiring strength and flexibility, whether tool handles, bows, spears, arrows or even the framework for early cars and aeroplanes. Before the introduction of hickory to the UK for hammers, these would have been given ash handles. The wood is also great for fire by friction, although it is a little tough. Ash plays host to cramp ball fungi (of which more on p.325).

Birch (Betula spp.)

There are two types of birch commonly found in the UK: the silver birch and the downy birch. They hybridise frequently, producing fertile offspring that can crossbreed with either parent plant. This makes specific identification quite tricky, although for our purposes, all of these birches can be used in the same way.

Fairly small, serrated, arrow-like leaves are key to identification of the species. The bark is often white in either of these two main species – don't be fooled into thinking that only the silver birch is white. This seems to have been an evolutionary response to the trees having grown in the open, probably aimed at reflecting light. In shady locations, the birch can adopt a coppery colour.

Both tar and oil can be obtained by dry distillation of birch bark (see Chapter 7), which also contains saponins – natural soaps that can be used when you're out in the woods. Birch is also an excellent tree for making withies (see Chapter 5).

The bark peels off readily and is a great firelighter, containing both fuel in the form of the bark and accelerant in the form of its oil. However, as mentioned previously, care must be taken when removing the bark, as it is all too easy to go too deep and damage the phloem – or energy transportation system – of the tree. Birch is a great wood for beginners to carve as it's reasonably tough but won't tax inexperienced hands.

Goat Willow (Salix caprea)

The goat willow (or pussy willow) is abundant in most British woodlands and, unlike other species of willow, does not require water to thrive. It also has notably unwillowlike leaves – much shorter, fatter and with a distinctive pinch and twist at the tip. Famously, willows contain salicylic acid, a key component of aspirin; this acid can be found in the inner bark.

The inner bark is great material for weaving and, when dead, makes ideal tinder. It also produces an excellent purple dye that can be used on cloth or to dye itself to make interesting-coloured weavers for basket work (see Chapter 7).

It's a medium-range, bow drill wood, but can season to be more like iron, so make sure that it is reasonably soft when harvesting.

Look out for the distinctive lenticels on the bark. The colour left behind when the bark is removed can be startling, albeit short-lived, and it is easy to imagine where the purple colour comes from.

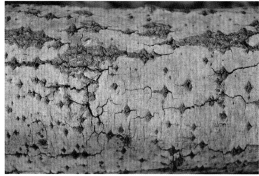

–2 (above and above right). Look for the twisted leaf tip and diamond-shaped lenticels on the bark.

. Dye can be obtained from the willow's bark.

Sycamore (Acer pseudoplatanus)

Although this is not a native tree, it is still extremely useful – one of the most wide-spread sources of bow drill wood in this country. It has a classic maple-shaped leaf with five lobes and these leaves are, as with all maples, arranged on opposite sides of the stem and alternating.

Opposite pairs of five-lobed leaves.

Sooty bark disease.

Sycamore frequently suffers from sooty bark disease, a fungus that seems to attack the phloem layer. I have found that trees suffering from this disease seem to be easier to make fire with. Look out for the classic black stains, which are revealed as the dead outer bark falls away. Sycamore wood is also fairly soft for carving, and therefore ideal for beginners.

Sweet Chestnut (Castanea sativa)
This tree is very distinctive, with large, spear-like leaves that are deeply serrated. Again, it is non-native and therefore of limited value for wildlife, but produces very dense, tough hardwood that is used traditionally for fencing – it is capable of remaining sound for twenty-five years or more.

From a bushcraft perspective, the bark is incredibly useful for both woven and folded containers, as well as for making string, and as tinder when dry and dead. Frequently, the outer bark rots away, leaving very dense heartwood that burns with great heat. However, it does spit – so care must be taken to protect important equipment and clothing. The wood splits readily and this – combined with its tannins, which protect it against rotting – is perhaps the reason for its popularity as fencing. It also produces an edible nut that is a wonderful autumn treat.

Lime (Tilia spp.)
There are three versions of this tree native to the UK: small-leaved, large-leaved and a naturally occurring hybrid of the two. All can be used in the same way, with lime being one of the easiest trees with which to make a bow drill fire.

These lime leaves are very young and great for eating.

300

The leaves are arranged in a very angular fashion, almost zigzagged along the stem. They often have a distinctive, large tip and are not generally symmetrical, with the lower lobes on the leaf rarely matching.

Together with willow, lime is the finest tree-based material for cordage that comes to mind. When the leaves are young, they are edible – which is not to imply that they become in any way toxic as they mature. It is just that later in the season they become stiff with cellulose, which humans can't digest. Lime leaves are also rich in mucilage, a slimy substance that is great for inflamed skin. Look for it as either rusty or white fur, where the veins meet the midrib on the back of the leaf.

Beech (Fagus sylvatica)

There is nothing more cathedral-like in nature than a forest of mature beech trees, which conjure an atmosphere all of their own. They are incredibly efficient at trapping light, so very little grows in their shade. Often confused with hornbeam, their oval, waxy leaves reveal a fluffy margin when held up to the light. Before they break, these leaves are rolled tightly in long, sharp, brown buds, the scales of which often remain on the tree throughout the growing season.

Beech tends to self-pollard and drop long lateral branches, an occurrence termed 'summer branch drop syndrome'. Therefore, it's advisable to avoid camping under these trees during calm, still days, which is when this is most likely to occur (see my description of long lateral branches on p.308). Their historic use mostly took advantage of the toughness of the wood.

ature beech leaves are hard and waxy; these are young nd have a slightly tangy taste.

To distinguish beech from hornbeam, look out for the woolly margin to the leaf.

Although not long-lasting outdoors, beechwood has been used tradition-ally in the manufacture of desks and kitchen surfaces. From a bushcraft perspective, beech makes incredibly hot-burning firewood.

Often, the wood can be found in a state of partial decay, with fungal decay lines known as spalting, which can be utilised for attractive craft-work. The tree is another host of the cramp ball fungus – an excellent source of tinder.

Hazel (Corylus avellana)

The true woodsman's friend, hazel is a tree that frequently looks coppiced even when it hasn't been, due to its multiple stems. The abun-dance of stems all growing up together, chasing the light, means that hazel lends itself to long, straight, often branch-free wands. These are ideal for a multi-tude of woodland uses: arrows, spears, the list goes on.

Look out for the distinct tip at the top of the hazel leaf.

A reasonably difficult bow drill wood, hazel can be so abundant and straight that it is hard to beat for the manufacture of drills. If you can catch them before the grey squirrels scoff the lot, the nuts are also available to a sharp-eyed forager. The leaves resemble lime, but on closer inspection the young twigs appear slightly furry.

Guelder Rose (Viburnum opulus)

This is a wonderful little shrub, native and highly prized by wildlife due to its succulent red berries in autumn. It has a wonderful autumn colour, turning deep red, and a flower so spectacular that you would think it doesn't belong on a British tree.

Don't confuse guelder rose with maple; its leaves have only three lobes.

Superficially, the guelder rose looks a little like a maple, but close inspection reveals a triple-lobed leaf with glands at the top of the leaf stalk. This is a prime source for primitive arrows. In fact, Ötzi the Iceman – who lived between 3400 and 3100 BCE, and whose mummified body was found trapped in a glacier in the Ötztal Alps – was found with a quiver of arrows made from our other native viburnum, the wayfaring tree: both of these plants have similar properties with regard to archery. In addition, guelder rose was used traditionally as a painkiller, and hence sometimes goes by the name 'cramp bark'.

Wych Elm (Ulmus glabra)
Like many elms, wych elm is under threat from Dutch elm disease. The leaves of this tree bear a resemblance to hazel, but when you run your thumb across their surface there is a rough, sandpapery quality that is distinctive of this species. The tiny buds should clinch any identification.

Wych elm, one of the Mesolithic bow woods.

The oldest bow in Europe was made from wych elm and the bark can be used for weaving – traditionally, it has been employed to make chair seats, as well as being a great material from which to make baskets. Rich in mucilage, the bark has been used historically as a food source in times of famine. When it is in flower, wych elm seeds are contained in a papery vessel that was also eaten.

Ten Tree Features Every Woodsman Should Know

Some of the features described below indicate danger but do remember that a tree shows these symptoms because it is dealing with the problem. The strategy is often successful, just as we are when dealing with an injury. *Please do not condemn every tree that is not the absolute picture of health.*

I include these features here for interest: my definition of bushcraft is to be able to walk through the woods and know what is going on. Note also that many of them provide vital habitats for a range of species.

Some of the features will give clues for navigation and many of the directional indicators mentioned in this section were first brought to my attention by the natural navigator Tristan Gooley, who is perhaps the world's foremost authority on this subject.

Bumps and Swellings

Unusual bumps or swellings on a tree may indicate a loss of internal structural integrity following decay. By destroying wood in one area, decay causes the tree to respond by putting on more wood to counteract the weakness.

Some of the most obvious of these features are visible on conifers, which suffer from the unflatteringly named bottle butt. The name comes from the shape formed as the tree suffering from conifer butt rot swells at the point of decay, and these fungi only attack the lower part of the tree. At the point where sound wood is found again, the tree takes on normal proportions. This leaves a shape very much like a wine bottle, clearly due to the lack of sound timber within the tree. The tree may be unsafe to be around, but bottle butt particularly limits your options should you wish to fell an afflicted tree, as cutting into trees with obvious swellings is extremely hazardous.

Burrs

Lumps and swellings can cause structures known as burrs. They have a variety of causes, with insects, bacteria or fungi triggering rapid and unstructured cell division in a specific area. Small burrs, or galls, found on twigs, fruit or leaves are usually caused by wasp larvae. The bigger burrs might resemble an untidy pile of sticks and twigs that looks like a very unconvincing bird's nest (known as witches' brooms) or a large, bowl-shaped lump on the side of the main trunk.

These lumps are exciting for a woodcraft enthusiast because rapid cell division causes a very funky grain. This grain reveals swirls and patterns not normally found in timber that, coupled with the usually rounded aspect of the burr or gall, makes for an ideal bowl or cup – the shallowest of which are known traditionally to woodsmen as noggins.

Right and below left: Unusual swellings may indicate decay within the tree.

Below right: This tree has given up completely.

Burrs may provide interesting craft pieces, but only take them from the trunk of a tree once it has been felled.

Removal of these structures causes huge damage to the tree, so make sure that either the branch containing the feature is removed entirely or, if the burr is on a trunk, that the tree is felled. Slowing down the drying process when you are working a noggin is also worth considering, as the unconventional grain pattern leads to unconventional drying patterns that may cause severe splits and cracks.

Long Lateral Branches

Long lateral branches are a great feature of which to be aware. As trees are phototropic, they can be a good indication of in which direction south lies, provided, of course, that the tree is either the biggest in the forest, or growing in the open. Where trees are desperately trying to escape the shade of other trees, long lateral branches may not point to the south.

Clockwise from top: The 'tick effect' can be noted when driving; Stimulated growth after felling exposes the tree and may also illustrate the direction of the sun.

Observing such trees should quite quickly illustrate this point, with the southern aspect of the crown being made up of much flatter branches and the northern aspect having much more steeply angled branches, as they try to reach over to catch the light. This is what Tristan Gooley, the excellent natural navigation specialist, calls 'the tick effect' in his book, *The Natural Navigator* (see Further Reading).

On some species, notably beech, long, heavy, lateral branches may be prone to breakage, often without warning. As mentioned previously, summer branch drop syndrome is not very well understood – at least in terms of its cause – but its effect can be very predictable if you happen to be camping underneath a beech tree at the wrong time. It seems most likely to occur on still, summer days – exactly at the time when you would think nothing should be dropping from the sky. Avoid working and certainly camping, under mature beech trees with long heavy lateral limbs in the summer.

Ribs

Ribs that are visible on the outside of a tree indicate internal structural weakening. They often consist of supporting wood that has grown over a split – a similar mechanism to the bulges compensating for the decay mentioned above. Once again, the tree has recognised a weakness, and attempts to build timber around it to regain structural integrity.

This feature is certainly worth considering when you pick a campsite. Rib-forming splits can be caused by a variety of stimuli, including lightning strikes and frost cracks, but perhaps the most common cause is torsion cracking, which often comes from an unbalanced crown. As a result of the imbalance, the tree suffers a severe twisting motion in high winds, almost as if it were trying to unwind itself.

Streaks and Folds

Streaks on the bark of a tree can be a cause for concern, as they may indicate structural weakness within it. What might be happening is that the tree, again sensing weakness and rapidly building around that weakness by producing more wood, is breaking through outer bark that is unable to keep up with the wood being produced underneath. This causes the bark to stretch and reveal fresh material.

Opposite: Ribs showing well on these mature birch trees.

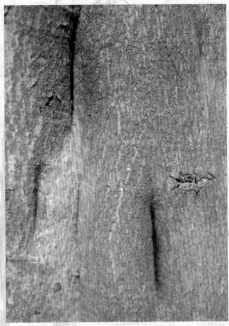

Above and right: Streaks and folds.

Below: Folds and swellings may indicate problems.

Folds in the bark of a tree, either in the main trunk or perhaps the underside of a branch, could be an indication that the timber is collapsing. The fibres might be giving way and causing a concertina effect in the wood.

Fallen Trees

Usually, the presence of lots of fallen trees, lying all in the same direction, is the result of a storm. Depending on where you are in the world, the direction that the storm is coming from is fairly consistent. In my neck of the woods, for example, most storms are westerly, thus most windblown trees in my local woods are on the ground with their root balls towards the west and the crown towards the east.

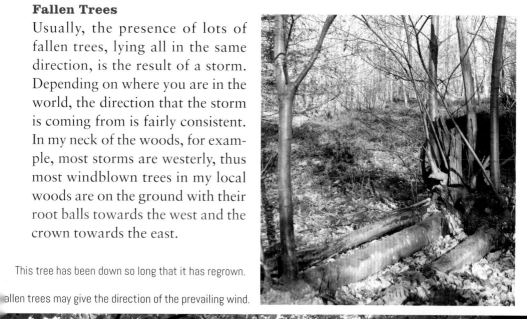

This tree has been down so long that it has regrown.

Fallen trees may give the direction of the prevailing wind.

Trees occasionally do face different directions so, as with all natural navigation indicators, it is important not to put all your faith in a single sign. Because of the regularity of storms, we have trees in all states of disarray. Some will still be propped up by other trees as a result of storms from two or three years ago, while others are on the ground, and others further still consist of just the root plates, often grown over and no longer attached to the trunk, which has long since rotted away. These little mounds in the wood are markedly longer than they are wide and run in a rough north–south line at their longest point.

Old Coppice Stools

Old coppice stools can help with direction-finding as they act like mini-forests, with each stem competing for light with the next. Therefore, it follows that stems on the south side tend to do better than those to the north. This can be seen even in stools that have long since died. Old stools from hardwoods may survive for decades to give an indication of past management.

Old coppice stools may give you direction. They certainly point to previous forest management.

This coppice stool has shaded out all the other stems o its root stock.

quirrel striping (left). By comparison, when a squirrel removes bark for nesting materials there are no evident gnaw
iarks (right)..

Squirrel Striping

Squirrels scent-mark trees by chewing through the outer bark, then rubbing
their scent there to let other squirrels know who is in the neighbourhood.
It is thought that the contrast in colour caused by this behaviour also acts
as a visual cue.

Most of these marks are made on the lee (sheltered) side of a tree, presumably to preserve the scent as long as possible, but I have not looked
at enough of them to be confident about how much this can be an aid for
direction-finding. Do let me know if you find examples and which way
they were facing!

Don't confuse striping activity with squirrels that have been gathering
nesting material: striping shows definite gnaw marks.

A tight fork after failure.

Tight Forks

When stems grow close together, racing each other for light, they may suffer weakness at the point where the base of the stems meet. Then, as they grow upwards, they increase in girth and, eventually, might push each other apart. The tree often responds by putting on more wood to reinforce this area.

The level of effort that the tree puts in to strengthening this area will determine how big these get. Particularly huge examples are referred to as 'elephant ears' – from a certain angle, they can stick out a remarkably long way. Tight forks can easily break out, especially when a tree is being felled.

Opposite: The tight fork of a beech tree showing the reinforcement of extra woo

314

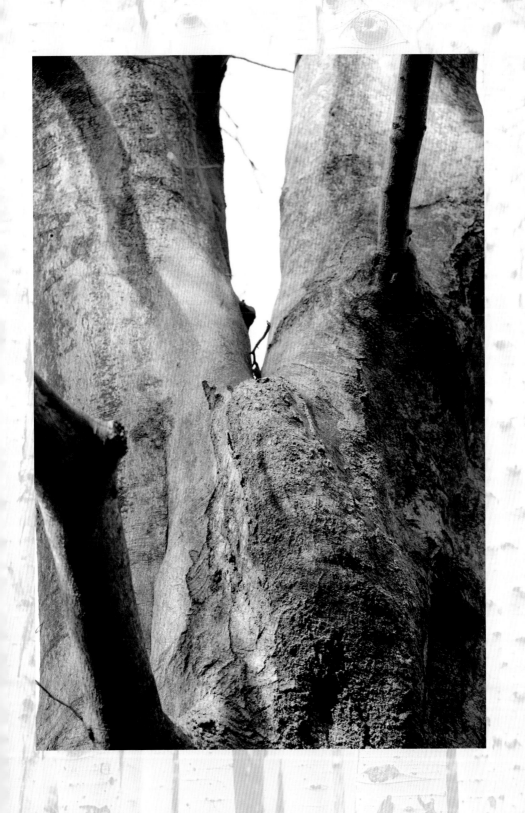

Clockwise from left: Sometimes roots are heavier on the windward side; Wind pruning is a reliable indication of direction; Another example of a strengthening root.

Wind Pruning

The prevailing wind can sculpt trees or groups of trees in a distinctive manner. Branches look as if they have been combed by the wind, and often slope up towards the lee (sheltered) side of the tree in a triangular shape. Trees also tend to have bigger roots on the windward side: buttress roots, especially, are usually there. Knowing the prevailing wind in an area can give you a very reliable indicator of direction.

Ten Fungi Every Woodsman Should Know

Hoof Fungus (Fomes fomentarius)

The best-known use for this fungus is as a fire-starter. Bracket fungi such as this have a layer of spore tubes underneath the bracket and immediately above the spongy layer known as the trama layer. It is this trama that forms the basis of fire-starting amadou, which is a material made by boiling and beating the trama to create a leather-like material. Often treated with saltpetre to enhance its ability to capture sparks, this prepared material burns like a fuse.

It burns well even without the added saltpetre, and as a completely dried fungi can be employed as a method of carrying fire. (In fact, this is true of many of the fungi described here.) Amadou has been used across a range of craft applications, including the manufacture of hats.

Horse hoof fungus.

As the name of the fungus suggests, it looks very much like the hoof of a horse. In the UK, hoof fungi can be found as far south as Norfolk and Suffolk, growing predominantly on birch. However, on the rare occasions when I have found this fungus in the south of England, it has been growing on beech. It is a very common fungus across Europe, often displacing the birch polypore (described next).

Birch Polypore (Fomitopsis betulina – Formerly Piptoporus betulinus)

Unlike hoof fungi, the birch polypore produces an annual bracket that, late in the season, rots away on the tree or dries. The fresh layer beneath the spore tubes can be peeled off and used as a sticking plaster. The trama can be removed and mounted on a block of wood to use as a strop to hone

Birch polypore.

blades, hence its other name: razor strop fungus. When dried, the whole thing works as a coal extender. It is also believed to have medicinal properties, effective against internal parasites such as whipworm.

Artist's Bracket (Ganoderma applanatum)

This is another great coal extender – there is definitely a theme here with bracket fungi – although the trama doesn't stay intact when trying to beat it out, unlike hoof fungi. It is still very useful when dried. Artist's bracket is being used to support cancer treatment, as are several other bracket fungi: this is a field of research that appears to offer some exciting possibilities.

When fresh, the underside of the fungus is a bright white colour, with layers of brown crusty material above. These are like the annual rings in

ist's bracket fungus.

The underside is so white that it can be drawn on.

These fungi can produce a huge number of spores.

trees, although there is often more than one growing phase in a twelve-month period, so it could be more accurate to call them biannual or even triannual rings. The underside is such a pure white that it can be drawn on, which may be the origin of its name. (I have heard that artists have used dried specimens of the fungus as a palette.)

True Tinder Fungus (Inonotus obliquus)

Also known as the chaga mushroom or true tinder mushroom, this fungus is often called the 'king of the medicinal mushrooms'. It certainly has a long history of use in healthcare across several cultures, and nowadays is available as a herbal supplement. (There seems to be evidence supporting at least some of its medicinal claims, although reading the marketing blurb, you would think there is nothing that it cannot do, perhaps even going so far as to confer the secret of immortality!)

The fungus grows predominantly on birch trees and looks like a piece of burnt wood. As its name suggests, it is an excellent coal extender.

True tinder or chaga fungus.

Turkey Tail (Trametes versicolor)

These fungi grow on dead stems and stumps, with their bands of contrast-ing colours making them look a bit like the raised tail of a turkey. Like all the fungi mentioned, they burn well when dried, but in medicinal terms there is strong evidence that turkey tail can boost the immune system. It has been used to support treatment for certain soft-tissue cancers, with scientific clinical trials supporting its effectiveness.

Chicken-of-the-Woods (Laetiporus sulphureus)

Sulphurous yellow when fresh, this fungus is frequently out and about in the late summer, when it positively glows in the deep shade of the wood-lands. Its flesh does indeed resemble the chicken that it is named after, and when young and tender it makes for a tasty, meaty meal. However, it does rapidly go woody and tasteless, and I know several people who react badly to eating it. On the plus side – and I'm sure you'll have guessed this bit – it burns well when dry.

Opposite and below: Turkey tail fungus.

Left and above: Chicken-of-the-woods.

Below: Dryad's saddle fungus.

Dryad's Saddle (Polyporus squamosus)

Another edible bracket fungus that appears in summer. In my region, I mostly find these growing on beech trees. They rapidly pass their sell-by date, with only the youngest and smallest worth gathering. Still, like chicken-of-the-woods, they will come out of the same tree or stump reliably, year-on-year. I haven't tried to burn them, but I would have pretty high hopes.

ramp balls.

Cramp Balls (Daldinia concentrica)

This is unmistakable, and probably the first utility fungus that a bushcraft student learns. It looks like a small burnt ball, which gives rise to its other name of King Alfred's cake – in honour of Alfred the Great, who allowed a swineherd's wife's cakes to burn while he was distracted, thinking about what to do with those pesky Vikings.

Excellent as a firelighter, cramp balls can be found in such quantities that they can be burnt like charcoal. In my region, I find them mostly on ash and beech trees, but I have found them also on willow, sycamore and, once, oak.

Beef Steak (Fistulina hepatica)

The jury is out on how tasty this mushroom is: some love it, but to others it is as bitter and repugnant as Satan's earwax. It looks very much like a slab of meat, complete with blood-like fluid. I find it predominantly growing on tannin-rich trees such as oak and sweet chestnut, which may account for its bitterness.

If the taste is too much for you, there are various recipes that make it more palatable – with boiling in milk a favourite method – but either way, I think young specimens would be the best place to start.

Wood afflicted by beef steak fungi frequently turns a rich colour, often in bands, and when I started in the woods, this was known as 'tiger oak' for that very reason.

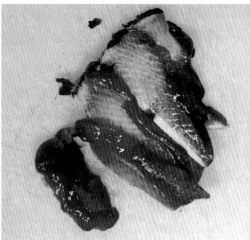

Above and right: Beef steak mushroom.

The wood that green cup fungi have grown on is turned a dramatic turquoise.

Green Cup Fungus (Chlorociboria aeruginascens)

I have included this one because, although it is so common, it is not widely recognised. It turns the wood on which it grows a vivid turquoise colour and, on a dull autumn day, the luminescence of the (seldom-found) fruiting body hurts the eyes. Because the fruiting body is rarely seen, most people mistake it for bits of old treated fencepost, but at one stage it was highly prized for inlays in Tunbridge ware. Regrettably, the fruiting bodies are so small that they are unlikely to be viable tinder.

9

Ropes and Knots

Nothing illustrates the need for a well-tied knot more than being forced to rely on it when things go slightly wrong. I well remember felling a group of huge alder trees that had overshadowed a small pond we were trying to restore. The trees were sitting back against the direction that I wanted them to go, so throwing a rope high into the canopy and tying a running bowline (as described below), I hooked up the rope to my trusty old Series 3 Land Rover. The sink cut and back cut – complete with gentle pressure from me – would bring the tree to the ground ... or so I thought.

Unfortunately, the tree sat back almost immediately, pulling the vehicle with it, and wouldn't budge. Hooking up a 4x4 pick-up to the front of my Land Rover, we tried again and succeeded only in sinking both cars up to the chassis in the mud.

By pulling the rope 90° to the direction of fall using a third vehicle, we finally managed to topple the tree. Clearly, to recover the vehicles we needed more horsepower, which we found in the form of Oliver the shire horse, who had the task of moving the timber around on this wet site, as his ground impact was a good deal less than that of a tractor.

Once hooked up to the cars, Oliver pulled them free with barely any effort. Throughout the whole experience, and despite tremendous strain, all our knots held and, just as importantly, we were able to undo the knots and use the rope to free the cars. If our knots had not been up to scratch, we might never have got home.

Ropes.

Working with ropes and tying knots has been part of my life for a very long time, both as an arborist and woodsman. There are lots of knots out there to choose from, but in this line of work only a few are ever needed. Throwing a rope is useful, fixing ends and making loops will be required, and a system of applying tension can be handy. Add the ability to join ropes together, and your repertoire is complete. If all these knots can be easily undone without resorting to a knife, so much the better.

Types of Rope

Ropes come in many guises and for myriad different uses – this can be quite confusing. It is worth spending a reasonable amount of money when getting a rope, especially for heavy tasks such as felling. The last thing you want is to have a rope break at the critical moment when you are trying to control a tree. It is worth spending money even when buying small-diameter rope, such as paracord.

There is a great deal of imitation paracord, which lacks the central core that gives the rope its strength. The good stuff has a braided outer layer containing several strands of nylon. There are also larger-diameter versions of this cord that superficially look the same, but I have had several lengths of this break. It seems that short lengths are joined together frequently using heat, which means that they break without warning, and with a suspiciously neat end.

I would avoid polypropylene rope, as it is very hard to coil, throw and generally make knots with; it is also likely to really tighten up under tension, making even undoable knots difficult to break open. Retired rock-climbing ropes can be useful, although they do stretch. Far better would be a non-dynamic – that is, not stretchy – tree surgeon's climbing rope. Specialist ropes used in tree work specifically for pulling trees and lowering branches can be bought, but these are quite expensive. I find the non-dynamic ropes used in sailing to be more than adequate for tree felling and general work around the woods.

Rope of 3/16–½in (11 or 12mm) diameter is a good size for general tree work, at least on the scale that we will be attempting. Having said that, there are some knots described below that won't work on large-diameter rope. Still, it can be useful to learn them on bigger ropes, because it makes the sequence easier to see.

Before we go any further, I need to introduce a couple of bits of terminology. I will be referring to the end of the rope with which we are making the knot as the 'working end', and the rest of it as the 'standing end'. Without wishing to upset the knot-tying fraternity, I use the term 'knot' and 'hitch' interchangeably, even though I am told that, technically speaking, a hitch is a knot that secures a rope to something solid, such as a tree.

1. First cross the working end over to form a loop (we refer to this as the 'rabbit's hole').
2. Take the rabbit around the standing end, now the tree, then back down the hole.
3. Hold the very end of the working end, now the rabbit, and pass it through the hole from underneath.
4. To tighten the knot, pull the rabbit and the tree.
5. Undoing a bowline knot.

Running bowline.

Types of Knot

Bowline

This is a great little knot to learn, as it gives you a loop that is great for tying round and pulling things. It's also a great knot for joining two lengths of rope together. The beauty of the bowline is the way it can be easily undone, even after having been put under tremendous strain. To undo the knot even after strain, it should be easy to push on the back of the knot as shown, to 'break' the knot.

Running Bowline

This is a variation on the standard bowline. The difference is that, before the rabbit comes out of the hole, it is first passed around the standing end. If this is thrown over a branch high in a tree to work as a felling aid, a running noose can be easily created.

The timber hitch process.

Above: A badly tied timber hitch will just unravel.

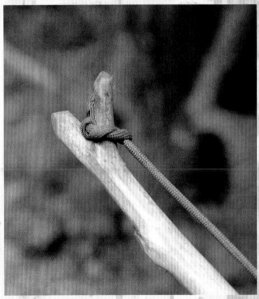

Left: A timber hitch being used on the bow drill.

Timber Hitch

This knot is a must for woodsmen. It can secure one end of the cord used on a bow drill yet is strong enough to attach to heavy timber that is to be dragged out of the wood. This hitch is also known as the bowyer's knot: it is traditionally used to secure the bowstring on the lower limb of a traditional bow.

1. Take the working end around the object to be secured. Loop over the standing end and bring it back onto itself to form an eye.

2. Wrap the working end back over itself a minimum of three times.

3. Spread these wraps out to give greater surface contact with the rope. This is important, as friction is the key component in making this hitch secure.

4. Slide and wiggle the standing end through the eye to tension. The most common mistake is to wrap the working end back in the wrong direction, not creating the eye.

Opposite and below: The half hitch.

Half Hitch

This set-up is immensely simple, yet very underrated. It can be used in conjunction with a timber hitch, especially when trying to secure something to a tree with smooth bark, where otherwise ropes might slip. The half-hitch can also be deployed in series and is potentially strong enough to pull vehicles, yet – just as with the timber hitch – comes easily undone as soon as the tension is released.

I frequently use a half-hitch to secure the other end of my bow drill string, finding three half-hitches a perfect number for this job. Although they will loosen eventually as you use the bow, the knots are very easy to undo and retie.

The half-hitch is a very easy knot to tie, as it consists of merely looping part of the rope across itself. Used in a series, the friction created is very high.

The carter's hitch sequence.

Carter's Hitch

Originally, the carter's (or wagoner's) hitch was used to secure loads to trailers and carts, hence the name. An enormous amount of tension can be generated with this knot, which makes it ideal for pulling trees over and for dragging them backwards or sideways, should they get hung up. I have used it to pull canoes up steep riverbanks, too.

The knot gives huge mechanical advantage and, if karabiners and strops are introduced, much of the friction generated by rope-on-tree or rope-on-rope is eliminated. This means that the ropes tend not to wear out, and the whole winching process is much more efficient.

1. Secure one end of the rope to whatever you need to move (in the case of tree felling), or fix the line to if just making a ridge line. A timber hitch or running bowline work well here. This secure point is known as the 'victim'.
2. Take the other end around a sturdy tree or other fixed point. This is called the 'anchor'.
3. Throw any excess rope over the part of the rope that will become the taut ridge.
4. From behind this point, gather a bite of rope and lay it across the ridge towards the victim, but beyond the point where you threw the excess over. A bite is like a loop of rope except a loop crosses itself and a bite merely touches.
5. Using part of the rope coming directly down from the victim, wrap a short piece to bind and form the loop into what is known as a 'dolly'.
6. Do this once more, putting this second piece behind the first, and lock it in. Use plenty of rope to create a loop below the dolly.

Because the locking rope was taken from behind the point where the rope was thrown over, the excess rope is captured within the loop. Picking this up and walking backwards should tension the knot. It can be tied off with a couple of half hitches, if required.

Reducing friction by using an eyed strop on the tree and a karabiner on the rope greatly increases efficiency.

Rolling Hitch

This is perhaps most useful indirectly, for tensioning guy lines. These can be employed in many ways in the woods, even if it's just something as simple as keeping a rope free of the ground. It can also be useful for creating a string keeper, which maintains a certain amount of tension on an unstrung bowstring. Often, this will prevent the string falling off the lower limb nock.

1   Using this knot as a guy line is perhaps the easiest way to learn it.

2. Take the end from your tent or tarpaulin and around an anchor.

3. Cross the working end over the standing end to create a figure 4 effect.

4. Wrap the working end through this figure 4, creating a coil, then do this again.

338

Rolling hitch sequence.

5. Next, take the working end around the standing end, but this time outside of the figure 4. This locks the whole thing down into a knot that can be slid to control the tension. (The knot in the illustration has been made slippery, to make untying easier – see below.)

Round Turn and Two Half Hitches
This can be used as an alternative to the timber hitch to provide a fixed end that is very strong and can be easily pulled against. It is perhaps used more frequently to secure the end of a tarpaulin or hammock when camping.

1. Secure your rope to a victim using a timber hitch or running bowline.

2. Walk the remainder around a secure anchor and throw the excess over the main ridgeline part of the rope.

3. Hook this back to form an eye, not unlike the timber hitch. This allows the working end to pull back against the anchor and produce great tension as the rope is walked around.

4. Two half-hitches can now be tied at the front of the anchor, securing the knot.

Making a Knot Slippery

All of the knots and hitches described above can be undone easily, but great strain – especially when using small-diameter cord – may make undoing them very tricky. To make a knot 'slippery', simply pull a loop through as illustrated, instead of the whole of the working end. This gives you something to pull against, should everything tighten up excessively.

he round turn and two half hitches sequence.

Throwing and Moving Ropes

Throwing a rope is an immensely useful skill: not only for aiding felling, but also for breaking out deadwood for fires, or keeping food out of harm's way. The sequence shown is a method developed for tree surgeons to enable them to gain access to canopy trees. I can think of no better way to throw a rope and still retrieve the end. For high throws, it is best to use a specific throwing line with a weighted bag, although in the forest is quite difficult not to lasso several trees this way.

1. Coil a few lengths of rope into your throwing hand – make these tight and small, no longer than your forearm. If they are too long, they will catch, and as this is to become the throwing weight, all the mass should be concentrated in a small area.

2. Be happy that you have enough rope in your bundle, which is determined by how much and how high you can throw. This bundle should come undone once it has gone over the branch.

3. The amount of rope coiled into the throwing bundle determines if the end of the rope can be reached or not.

4. The bundle can be finished off by wrapping a half-turn around the coils and pulling a loop through. This becomes the handle, which should still be held in the throwing hand.

5. Next, place further small coils into the same hand as travel. This provides enough rope to be able the reach the target.

6. Now, you are ready to throw the whole lot over the chosen branch. (I find it best to do this overhand, like bowling a cricket ball; I also find it easier to hold extra travel in my non-throwing hand.)

Opposite: A slippery bowline.

Above and opposite: Making the throwing bundle sequence.

Sometimes you might throw a rope over a convenient limb but be unable to reach it, or it might get stuck. For most people, the first instinct is to engage in some ineffectual flicking of the rope. What needs to happen is for more rope to be sent up the tree and over the limb, as illustrated. Start fairly close to the tree and make a loop in the rope that is large enough to almost touch the ground. This loop is then sent up and over the branch by vigorous bowling of your arm. By flicking your arm left or right as the rope is bowled, it can be moved right or left along branches surprisingly effectively. This is great when hanging food or looking for the leverage to break out some deadwood.

Bowling the rope sequence.

Further Reading

Abbot, M., *Green Woodwork: Working with Wood the Natural Way* (1989).

Baker, T., and P. Comstock, *The Traditional Bowyer's Bible*, Vol. 4 (2015).

Claus, M., *Stupsi Explains the Tree: A Hedgehog Teaches the Body Language of Trees* (1999).

Congreve, Lady C., 'The Firewood Poem', *The Times* (2 March 1930).

Flint, I., *Eco Colour: Botanical Dyes for Beautiful Textiles* (2008).

Goodhart, H., 'Logs to Burn', *Punch* (27 October 1920). Available from: http://pond1.gladstonefamily.net/logs-to- burn.html (accessed 18 January 2018).

Gooley, T., *The Natural Navigator: The Art of Reading Nature's Own Signposts* (2014).

Gooley, T., *The Walker's Guide to Outdoor Clues & Signs* (2015).

Hamm, J., *The Traditional Bowyer's Bible*, Vols 1–3 (2000).

Hardy, R., *Longbow: A Social and Military His tory* (1992).

Langsner, D., *Green Woodworking: A Hands-On Approach* (1995).

Law, B., *Woodland Craft* (2017).

Wescott, D. (ed.), *Primitive Technology: A Book of Earth Skills* (1999).

Wescott, D., *Primitive Technology II: Ancestral Skills* (2001).

Index